ALL ABOUT SEX

ALL
ABOUT
SEX

Compiled by Peter Potter

A
BULL'S-EYE

BOOK

Published by
William Mulvey Inc.
72 Park Street
New Canaan, Conn. 06840

Cover design: Ted Palmer

Library of Congress Cataloging-in-Publication Data

All About Sex
"A Bull's-eye Book"

Includes index.
1. Sex—Quotations, maxims, etc.   I. Potter, Peter (date).
II. Series: All About (New Canaan, CT).

PN6084.S49A45   1988   081   86-90384

ISBN 0-934791-04-X

Printed in the United States of America
First Edition

To
my Family,
for their encouraging support

Introduction

Sex. Sex. Sex. The world at times seems to be preoccupied with it. Television, movies, newspapers, magazines, books. Sex sells.

At parties. In the office. On the street. Yes, even in the home. Sex is there, you can't get away from it.

Has it always been this way? Well, it's been around a long time. Starting with The Bible.

What's it all about, anyway?

Here's what the great thinkers of the world say about Sex. Here's what popular people of today—some quite experienced— say about Sex.

Read on. Learn. Enjoy.

Peter Potter

A

Activity, Sexual

Adeptness

Adultery

Affairs

Affection

Age, Men's

Age, Women's

Aging

Ambiguity

Animal-Like Behavior

Arguments

Attraction

Activity, Sexual

A Frenchwoman, when double-crossed, will kill her rival; the Italian woman would rather kill her deceitful lover; the Englishwoman simply breaks off relations—but they all will console themselves with another man.

Charles Boyer

If it weren't for pickpockets I'd have no sex life at all.

Rodney Dangerfield

People's sex habits are as known in Hollywood as their political opinions, and much less criticized.

Ben Hecht

All love scenes started on the set are continued in the dressing room.

Alfred Hitchcock

(Sex is) a perfectly normal, almost commonplace, activity. . . of the same nature as dancing or tennis.

Aldous Huxley

The important thing in acting is to be able to laugh and cry. If I have to cry, I think of my sex life. If I have to laugh, I think of my sex life.

Glenda Jackson

—————

When a man says he had pleasure with a woman he does not mean conversation.

Samuel Johnson

—————

Your sexuality is a dimension of your personality, and whenever you are sexually active, you are expressing yourself—the self that you are at that moment, the mood that you're in, the needs that you have.

Virginia Johnson

—————

Women complain about sex more often than men. Their gripes fall into two major categories: (1) Not enough. (2) Too much.

Ann Landers

—————

God forbid that I should be taken as urging loose sex activity. There is a brief time for sex, and a long time when sex is out of place. But when it is out of place as an activity there still should be the large and quiet place in the consciousness, where it lives quiescent. Old people can have a lovely quiescent sort of sex, like apples, leaving the young free for their sort.

D.H. Lawrence

You come out of a woman and you spend the rest of your life trying to get back inside.

Heathcote Williams

If you aren't going all the way, why go at all?

Joe Namath

I'll canvas thee between a pair of sheets.

Shakespeare

Adeptness

The majority of husbands remind me of an orangutan trying to play the violin.

Honoré de Balzac

In love-making, as in the other arts, those do it best who cannot tell how it is done.

James M. Barrie

Husbands are chiefly good lovers when they are betraying their wives.

Marilyn Monroe

What I hate is the girl who gives with a feeling she
    has to,
Dry in the bed, with her mind somewhere else, gathering
    wool.

Ovid

There are two things no man will admit he can't do well: drive
and make love.

Stirling Moss

I sometimes sleep with other girls in boudoir or cheap joint,
With energy and tenderness trying not to disappoint.
So do not think of helpful whores as aberrational blots;
I could not love you half so well without my practice shots.

James Simmons

It's not the men in my life that counts—it's the life in my men.

Mae West

Adultery

A man may commit adultery with a woman knowing well who
she is, but not of free choice, because he is under the influence of passion. In that case he is not an unjust man, though
he has done an injustice.

Aristotle

To keep thee from the evil woman, from the flattery of the tongue of a strange woman,

Lust not after her beauty in thine heart; neither let her take thee with her eyelids.

For by means of a whorish woman a man is brought to a piece of bread: and the adulteress will hunt for the precious life.

Can a man take fire in his bosom, and his clothes not be burned?

Can one go upon hot coals, and his feet not be burned?

So he that goeth in to his neighbor's wife; whosoever toucheth her shall not be innocent.

The Bible

I look with horror upon adultery, But my amiable mistress is no longer bound to him who was her husband. He has used her shockingly ill. He has deserted her. He lives with another. Is she not then free? She is.

James Boswell

What men call gallantry, and gods adultery,
Is much more common when the climate's sultry.

George Gordon Byron

It shall be considered adultery to offer presents to a married woman, to romp with her, to touch her dress or ornaments, or to sit with her on a bed.

Laws of Manu

Four things does a reckless man gain who covets his neighbor's wife—a bad reputation, an uncomfortable bed, thirdly punishment, and lastly hell.

> Dhammapada

Other people's wives are always the best.

> Chinese proverb

Do not adultery commit;
Advantage rarely comes of it.

> Arthur Hugh Clough

Adultery: For persons to dream they have committed it shows that they shall meet great contentions and debates; but to dream they have resisted the temptation to it shows victory over their enemies, and that they shall escape great dangers.

> Dictionary of the Interpretation of Dreams

Adultery can be a more 'healthy' recreation than for example the game of Mah Jongg or watching television.

> Albert Ellis

When cheated, wife or husband feels the same.

> Euripides

If they had as much adultery going on in New York as they said in the divorce courts, they. . .would never have a chance to make the beds at the Plaza.

Zsa Zsa Gabor

When dealing with adultery becomes a matter of private choice instead of public rules, middle-class morality, that bastion of social stability, has ceased to function.

Elizabeth Janeway

To set your neighbor's bed a shaking. . .an ancient and long-established custom.

Juvenal

Adultery is extravagance.

Maxine Hong Kingston

There is nothing which Allah abhors more than adultery. The eye and the tongue can commit adultery.

The Koran

(Adultery is) usually an act done under cover of darkness and secrecy, and in which the parties are seldom surprised.

Maryland Court of Appeals

Against those of your women who commit adultery, call witnesses four in number from among yourselves; and if these bear witness, then keep the women in houses until death release them or God shall make for them a way.

The Koran

. . .one of the most frequent causes of adultery: the longing a transparent man feels to become opaque. He suddenly finds himself wrapped in mystery, as if he had bought a new suit. This mystery is most becoming; it conceals the fact that the left shoulder is lower than the right, it nips in the waist, it makes the leg more slender. Oh, it's a marvelous tailor! The unexpected new suit makes you look fifteen years younger.

Jean Dutourd

But when they are married, if they commit fornication, then inflict upon them half the penalty for married women; that is for whomsoever of you fears wrong; but that ye should have patience is better for you, and God is forgiving and merciful.

The Koran

Men who commit adultery with the wives of others, the king shall cause to be marked by punishments which cause terror and afterwards banish.

Laws of Manu

An adulterer: He tills another's field and leaves his own untended.

Plautus

For by adultery is caused a mixture of the castes among men, thence follows sin, which cuts up even the roots and causes the destruction of everything.

Laws of Manu

(Adultery is) the application of democracy of love.

Henry Louis Mencken

'Come, come', said Tom's father, 'at your time of life,
  'There's no longer excuse for thus playing the rake—
'It is time you should think, boy, of taking a wife'—
  'Why, so it is, father—whose wife shall I take?'

Sturge Moore

(Adultery is) the great democratic vice.

George Bernard Shaw

The way of the adulterer is hedged with thorns; full of fears and jealousies, burning desires and impatient waitings, tediousness of delay and suffrance of affronts, and amazements of discovery.

Jeremy Taylor

The Bishops are trying to put a stop to one staple commodity of that kind, adultery. I do not suppose that they expect to lessen it.

Horace Walpole

Affairs

Little affairs may be useful for many reasons, including the opportunity to replace lovers who have contributed sexual dissonance with others more able to contribute consonance.

Jean Baer

I wouldn't be surprised (if her daughter had an affair). I think she's a perfectly normal human being like all young girls. If she wanted to continue, I would certainly counsel and advise her on the subject. And I'd want to know pretty much about the young man. . . She's pretty young to start affairs, (but) she's a big girl.

Betty Ford

I feel very angry when I think of brilliant, or even interesting women whose minds are wasted on a home. Better have an affair. It isn't so permanent and you keep your job.

John Kenneth Gailbraith

To be very frank for a moment, the extra-matrimonial love affair has never struck me as so much an offense against religion, or a violation of what "the new morality" calls "sex-taboos," as a breach of that loyalty and good faith that one partner expects of another under every other contract.

Channing Pollock

You are suggesting I have some sort of romantic attachment. I have no relationship with her, just a passing acquaintance for two nights.

Mick Jagger,
on Margaret Trudeau

⸻

I think a man can have two, maybe three love affairs while he is married. But three is the absolute maximum. After that you are cheating.

Yves Montand

⸻

God is a maker of marriages, but I wonder if He would bother to come to some of the affairs He has arranged.

Harry Golden

⸻

I can understand companionship. I can understand bought sex in the afternoon. I cannot understand the love affair.

Gore Vidal

⸻

When he is late for dinner and I know he must be either having an affair or lying dead in the street, I always hope he's dead.

Judith Viorst

⸻

A secret love affair is much more enjoyable than an open one.

Paulus Silentiarius

Affection

It's not till sex has died out between a man and a woman that they can really love. And now I mean affection. Now I mean to be fond of (as one is fond of oneself)—to hope, to be disappointed, to live inside the other heart. When I look back on the pain of sex, the love like a wild fox so ready to bite, the antagonism that sits like a twin beside love, and contrast it with affection, so deeply unrepeatable, of two people who have lived a life together (and of whom one must die) it's the affection I find richer. It's that I would have again. Not all those doubtful rainbow colours. (But then she's old, one must say.)

Enid Bagnold

When you put a man and a woman together, there are some things they simply have to do. They embrace. They warm each other. All the rest is dead and empty.

Ugo Betti

Sex without antecedent affection in the primate is a dim and gloomy thing.

Harry Harlow

A diamond is the only kind of ice that keeps a girl warm.

Elizabeth Taylor

Age, Men's

The French are true romantics. They feel the only difference between a man of forty and one of seventy is thirty years of experience.

Maurice Chevalier

A man loses his illusions first, his teeth second, and his follies last.

Helen Rowland

A lecherous old man is intolerable.

Talmud

The male sex, as a sex, does not universally appeal to me. I find the men today less manly; but a woman of my age is not in a position to know exactly how manly they are.

Katharine Hepburn

A man is only as old as the woman he feels.

Groucho Marx

When I was young, I used to have successes with women because I was young. Now I have successes with women because I am old. Middle age was the hardest part.

Arthur Rubinstein

The big mistake that men make is that when they turn 13 or 14 and all of a sudden they've reached puberty, they believe that they like women. Actually, you're just horny. It doesn't mean you like women any more at 21 than you did at 10.

Jules Feiffer

Age, Women's

In various stages of her life, a woman resembles the continents of the world. From 13 to 18, she's like Africa—virgin territory, unexplored; from 18 to 30, she's like Asia—hot and exotic; from 30 to 45, she's like America—fully explored and free with her resources; from 45 to 55, she's like Europe—exhausted, but not without places of interest; after 55, she's like Australia—everybody knows it's down there but nobody much cares.

Al Boliska

A woman's always younger than a man
At equal years.

Elizabeth Barrett Browning

Better be an old man's darling than a young man's slave.

English proverb

The years that a woman subtracts from her age are not lost. They are added to other women's.

Diane de Poitiers

There are more well-pleased old women than old men.

Richard Steele

Aging

Aging induces some changes in human sexual performance. These are chiefly in the male, for whom orgasm becomes less frequent. It occurs in every second act of intercourse, or in one act in three, rather than every time. More direct physical stimulation is also needed to produce an erection. However, compared with, say, running ability, these changes are functionally minimal and actually tend in the direction of "more miles per gallon" and greater, if less acute, satisfaction for both partners. In the absence of two disabilities—actual disease and the belief that "the old" are or should be asexual—sexual requirement and sexual capacity are lifelong. Even if and when actual intercourse is impaired by infirmity, other sexual needs persist, including closeness, sensuality and being valued as a man or as a woman.

Alex Comfort

The shame of aging is not that Desire should fail (who mourns for something he no longer needs?): it is that someone else must be told.

W.H. Auden

17

Love is the word used to label the sexual excitement of the young, the habituation of the middle-aged, and the mutual dependence of the old.

John Ciardi

O glorious boon of age, if it does indeed free us from youth's most vicious fault.

Marcus Tullius Cicero

The only thing age has to do with sex performance is that the longer you love, the more you learn.

Alex Comfort

It is the fear of middle-age in the young, of old-age in the middle-aged, which is the prime cause of infidelity, that infallible rejuvenator.

Cyril Connolly

A one-time U.S. Ambassador in Europe, astonishing in view of his age, is said to have approached all problems with a closed mind and an open fly.

John Kenneth Gailbraith

Quite a few women told me, one way or another, that they thought it was sex, not youth, that's wasted on the young. . .

Janet Harris

How well I remember the aged poet, Sophocles, when in answer to the question, "How does love suit your age—are you still the man you were?" replied, "Peace, most gladly have I escaped the thing of which you speak; I feel as if I had escaped from a mad and furious master!"

Plato

Adultery brings on early old age.

Hebrew proverb

I find that the three major administrative problems on a campus are sex for the students, athletics for the alumni, and parking for the faculty.

Clark Kerr

Ambiguity

The act of sex, gratifying as it may be, is God's joke on humanity. It is man's last desperate stand at superintendency.

Bette Davis

Sex is. There is nothing more to be done about it. Sex builds no roads, writes no novels and sex certainly gives no meaning to anything in life but itself.

Gore Vidal

There may be some things better than sex, and some things may be worse. But there is nothing exactly like it.

W.C. Fields

———

(Sex is) an irresistible attraction and an overwhelming repugnance and disgust.

George Bernard Shaw

———

(Sex is) a breeder of diseases, a gall to the conscience, a corrosive to the heart.

John Taylor

———

(Sex is) the body's bane, and the soul's perdition.

John Taylor

———

(Sex is) a short pleasure, bought with long pain, a honeyed poison, a gulf of shame.

John Taylor

———

Next to the wound, what women make best is the bandage.

Barbey D'Aurevilly

Animal-Like Behavior

Always remember: after ten o'clock a man becomes a beast.
Anonymous

A woman is but an animal, and an animal not of the highest order.
Edmund Burke

The ability to make love frivolously is the chief characteristic which distinguishes human beings from the beasts.
Heywood Broun

With the great majority of animals. . .the taste for the beautiful is confined, as far as we can judge, to the attractions of the opposite sex.
Charles Darwin

They made love as though they were an endangered species.
Peter de Vries

It is not human "to act the beast," to deify sexuality and set it up as an absolute. Raw sexual appetite is no more a sign of love than violence and brutality are signs of strength.

Henri Gilbert

Below the navel there is neither religion nor truth.

Italian proverb

What they call "heart" is located far lower than the fourth waistcoat button.

G.C. Lichtenberg

Most human sexual behavior is learned. It is only in the lower animals that it is totally instinctive. The higher on the evolutionary scale you are, the less instinctive are your sexual relations. So our life experiences "teach" us our sexuality, which may turn out to be hetero, homo, or bi.

Del Martin

Because the human self is a person (not just a body), marital intercourse must be a communion of persons, a loving personal exchange. To the extent that actual sexual intimacy recedes from the personal, to that extent it ceases to be an act of love and approximates more closely to the mating of mere animals.

Richard A. McCormick

The oddest of all the animals is man; in him, as in other animals, the sexual interest is the strongest, yet the desire is inveterate in him to reject it.

George Moore

In the friendship of the lover there is no real kindness; he has an appetite and wants to feed upon you. "Just as the wolf loves the lamb, so the lover adores his beloved."

Plato

Human beings are not animals, and I do not want to see sex and sexual differences treated as casually and amorally as dogs and other beasts treat them. I believe this could happen under the ERA.

Ronald Reagan

Although man has learned through evolution to walk in an upright position, his eyes still swing from limb to limb.

Margaret Schooley

When passion breaks away from the deep life of a man it can never enlarge him, it has nothing to say to the heart; it can never be a marriage of gods, only an animal mauling its prey.

Gerald Vann

Arguments

With women, men are the enemy; they abuse them as a nation abuses a people with whom it is at war, with old stories told in other wars.

Ed Howe

Nothing can vex
Like the opposite sex.

Georgie Starbuck Galbraith

Sex is not only a divine and beautiful activity, it's a murderous activity. People kill each other in bed. Some of the greatest crimes ever committed were committed in bed. And no weapons were used.

Norman Mailer

The only way to resolve a situation with a girl is to jump on her and things will work out.

Lee Marvin

All possibility of understanding is rooted in the ability to say no.

Susan Sontag

A woman's place is in the wrong.

James Thurber

Attraction

A good actress lasts, but sex appeal does not.

Brigitte Bardot

What a woman most admires in a man is distinction among
men.
What a man most admires in a woman is devotion to himself.

Ambrose Bierce

Not a strawberry there was so ripe nor so
sweet
As the lips which I kiss'd to subdue your
alarms.

Robert Bloomfield

If a man hears much that a woman says, she is not beautiful.

Anonymous

Unless a woman has an amorous heart, she is a dull com-
panion.

Samuel Johnson

Men aren't attracted to me by my mind. They're attracted by
what I don't mind.

Gypsy Rose Lee

One of the paramount reasons for staying attractive is so you can have somebody to go to bed with.

Helen Gurley Brown

Man is the head, but woman turns it.

Cheshire proverb

He was close on to six feet tall, of military bearing and of such extraordinary vitality that young ladies asserted they could feel him ten feet away.

C. Hartley Grattan

Sex appeal is 50 percent what you've got and 50 percent what people think you've got.

Sophia Loren

To the average male there is seemingly nothing so attractive or so challenging as a reasonably good-looking young mother who is married and alone.

Shirley MacLaine

Love may or may not include sexual attraction. It may express itself in sexual desire. But sexual desire is not love. Desire is quite compatible with personal hatred, or contempt, or indifference.

John MacMurray

A mutual sexual attraction is no proper basis for a human relationship between a man and a woman. It is an organic thing, not personal.

John MacMurray

———

. . .it is not so much modesty as artfulness and prudence that makes our ladies so circumspect in refusing us entry to their boudoirs before they are painted and dressed up for public display.

Michel de Montaigne

———

I know many married men; I even know a few happily married men; but I don't know one who wouldn't fall down the first open coal-hole running after the first pretty girl who gave him a wink.

George Jean Nathan

———

And here's the happy bounding flea—
You cannot tell the he from she.
But she can tell and so can he.

Roland Young

———

As the man beholds the woman,
    As the woman sees the man,
Curiously they note each other,
    As each other only can.

Bryan Waller Procter

An absence, the decline of a dinner invitation, an unintentional coldness, can accomplish more than all the cosmetics and beautiful dresses in the world.

Marcel Proust

A man's sexual choice is the result and sum of his fundamental convictions. Tell me what a man finds sexually attractive and I will tell you his entire philosophy of life.

Ayn Rand

Hair is another name for sex.

Vidal Sassoon

Being baldpate is an unfailing sex magnet.

Telly Savalas

It is better to be looked over than overlooked.

Mae West

In the argot of the sub-deb, "U.S.A."has long ago lost its patriotic meaning. It now stands for "Universal Sex Appeal."

Mary Day Winn

B

Beating
Beauty
Bisexuality
Breasts

Beating

I don't think there's anything wrong about hitting a woman—although I don't recommend doing it in the same way you'd hit a man. An open-handed slap is justified—if all other alternatives fail and there has been plenty of warning.

Sean Connery

A woman, a dog, and a walnut-tree,
The more you beat 'em the better they be.

Thomas Fuller

A gentleman is one who never strikes a woman without provocation.

H.L. Mencken

Beauty

The trouble with life is that there are so many beautiful women and so little time.

John Barrymore

Most women are not so young as they are painted.

Max Beerbohm

The loveliest and purest of God's creatures, the nearest thing to an angelic being that treads this terrestrial ball, is a well-bred, cultured, Southern white woman, or her blue-eyed, golden-haired little girl.

Judge Thomas P. Brady

You should be more concerned with being lovely than being loved.

A. Berggren

Beauty is a very handy thing to have, especially for a woman who ain't handsome.

Josh Billings

Why did he marry that Jackie? She is ugly, with horrible legs, the skin of a hen, fat in the wrong places, and eyes too far apart from one another. She's a big nothing.

Litsa Calogeropoulos
(Maria Callas' mother)

Love makes a spot beautiful; who chooses not to dwell in love, has he got wisdom?

Confucius

It's a good thing that beauty is only skin-deep, or I'd be rotten to the core.

Phyllis Diller

Woman . . . cannot be content with health and agility: she must make exorbitant efforts to appear something that never could exist without a diligent perversion of nature. Is it too much to ask that woman be spared the daily struggle for superhuman beauty in order to offer it to the caresses of a subhumanly ugly mate?

Germaine Greer

If I told you you have a beautiful body, you wouldn't hold it against me would you?

David Fisher

When men meet they listen; when women meet they look.

German proverb

The human knee is a joint and not an entertainment.

Percy Hammond

With those delicate features of his he would have made a pretty woman, and he probably never has.

Josefa Heifetz

Endless commercials and television programs show the lovable woman as a cuddly, soft, yielding girl-child sex object, with hair that bounces, lips that invite deep kisses, a body that smells like heavenly spring.

Clare Boothe Luce

Plain women know more about men than beautiful ones.

Katharine Hepburn

———

Gentlemen prefer blondes, but take what they can get.

Don Herold

———

I'm tired of all this nonsense about beauty being only skin-deep. That's deep enough. What do you want—an adorable pancreas?

Jean Kerr

———

How many girls are there for whom great beauty has been of no use but to make them hope for a great fortune?

Jean de La Bruyère

———

Beauty in a woman's face, like sweetness in a woman's lips, is a matter of taste.

Mary Wilson Little

———

She always believed in the old adage, "Leave them while you're looking good."

Anita Loos

———

She got her good looks from her father—he's a plastic surgeon.

Groucho Marx

Think first ye woman, to look at your behavior. The face pleases when character commends. Love of character is lasting; beauty will be ravaged by age.

Ovid

Every girl should use what Mother Nature gave her before Father Time takes it away.

Laurence J. Peter

When the candles are out all women are fair.

Plutarch

The new bold beauty is round; she is not scrawny. She's sexy, earthy. She has fire and excitement in her eyes. Her body looks healthy, and strong enough so you could wrestle and roll with her.

Francesco Scavullo

The eyes of men love to pluck the blossoms; from the faded flowers they turn away.

Sophocles

She was a Phantom of delight
When first she gleamed upon my sight;
A lovely Apparition sent
To be a moment's ornament.

William Wordsworth

If truth is beauty, why don't women get their hair done in the library?

Lily Tomlin

A curved line is the loveliest distance between two points.

Mae West

Of two evils choose the prettier.

Carolyn Wells

Bisexuality

I'm a practicing heterosexual. . . but bi-sexuality immediately doubles your chances for a date on Saturday night.

Woody Allen

I sleep with men and with women. I am neither queer nor not queer, nor am I bisexual.

Allen Ginsberg

There never lived a woman who did not wish she were a man. There never lived a man who wished he were a woman.

E.W. Howe

I had reached the conclusion myself that sex was not a division but a continuum, that almost nobody was altogether of one sex or another, and that the infinite subtlety of the shading from one extreme to the other was one of the most beautiful of nature's phenomena. Sex was like a biological pointer, but the gauge upon which it flickered was that very different device, gender.

Jan Morris

Bisexuality is not so much a copout as a fearful compromise.

Jill Johnston

I haven't met anybody I'd like to settle down with—of either sex.

Elton John

Psychic bisexuality is a de-conditioning process, which can eventually eliminate sexist limitations for both men and women.

Charlotte Painter

What is most beautiful in virile men is something feminine; what is most beautiful in feminine women is something masculine.

Susan Sontag

Different though the sexes are, they intermix. In every human being a vacillation from one sex to the other takes place, and often it is only the clothes that keep the male or female likeness, while underneath the sex is the very opposite of what it is above.

Virginia Woolf

I believe that bisexuality is almost a necessary factor in artistic production. . .

Muriel Rukeyser

Breasts

She (Elizabeth Taylor) is an extremely beautiful woman, lavishly endowed by nature with but a few flaws in the masterpiece: she has an insipid double chin, her legs are too short, and she has a slight pot-belly. She has a wonderful bosom, though.

Richard Burton

The only place men want depth in a woman is in her décolletage.

Zsa Zsa Gabor

If half the engineering effort and public interest that go into the research on the American bosom had gone into our guided-missile program, we would now be running hot-dog stands on the moon.

Al Capp

A full bosom is actually a millstone around a woman's neck: it endears her to the men who want to make their mammet of her, but she is never allowed to think that their popping eyes actually see her. . . (Breasts) are not parts of a person but lures slung around her neck, to be kneaded and twisted like magic, putty, or mumbled and mouthed like lolly ices.

Germaine Greer

The mammary fixation is the most infantile—and most American—of the sex fetishes. . .

Molly Haskell

What would they do with the chest protectors? Rebuild them all?

Early Wynn, pitching coach for the Minnesota Twins, on the attempts of a New York woman to get a job as umpire in the major leagues, 1968.

C

Celibacy
Censorship
Chastity
Chauvinism, Male
Children
Civilization
Clothing
Compatibility
Communication
Competition
Conquest
Continence
Contraception
Cultural Differences

Celibacy

Psychoanalysis has at last shown what all decent and clean-minded people knew about prolonged sexual abstinence—that it is both wrongful and harmful.

Anthony Ludovici

The advantage of being celibate is that when one sees a pretty girl one needs not grieve over having an ugly one back home.

Paul Leautaud

Marriage has many pains but celibacy has no pleasures.

Samuel Johnson

As to marriage or celibacy, let a man take which course he will, he will be sure to repent.

Socrates

I go out with actresses because I'm not apt to marry one.

Henry Kissinger

Censorship

The sooner we all learn to make a distinction between disapproval and censorship, the better off society will be. . . Censorship cannot get at the real evil, and it is an evil in itself.

Granville Hicks

I am going to introduce a resolution to have the Postmaster General stop reading dirty books and deliver the mail.

Gale McGee

Any country that has sexual censorship will eventually have political censorship.

Kenneth Tynan

Chastity

Set chastity above life itself.

Aeschylus

A salamander is a kind of heroine in chastity that treads upon fire and lives in the midst of flames, without being hurt.

Joseph Addison

44

The virtue of chastity most of all makes man apt for contemplation, since sexual pleasures most of all weigh the mind down to sensible objects.

Saint Thomas Aquinas

A reputation for chastity is necessary to a woman. Chastity itself is also sometimes useful.

Anonymous

Lord give me chastity—but not yet.

Saint Augustine

Chaste men engender obscene literatures.

Ausonius

Chaste women are often proud and forward, as presuming upon the merit of their chastity.

Francis Bacon

The most virtuous woman always has something within her that is not quite chaste.

Honoré de Balzac

Is not chastity a virtue? Most undoubtedly, and a virtue of high deserving. And why? Not because it diminishes, but because it heightens enjoyment.

Jeremy Bentham

Be warm, but pure; be amorous, but be chaste.

George Gordon Byron

Chastity and Beauty, which were deadly foes, Live reconciled friends within her brow.

Samuel Daniel

Chastity, the lily of virtues, makes men almost equal to angels. Nothing is beautiful but what is pure, and the purity of men is chastity.

Saint Francis de Sales

The chaste, they love not vice of their own will, but yet they love it.

Euripides

Banish all objects of lust, shut up all youth into the severest discipline that can be exercised in any hermitage, ye cannot make them chaste, that came not thither so.

John Milton

Chastity more rarely follows fear, or a resolution, or a vow, than it is the mere effect of lack of appetite and, sometimes even, of distaste.

André Gide

Of all sexual aberrations, chastity is the strangest.

Anatole France

Chastity is the most unnatural of the sexual perversions.

Rémy de Gourmont

We have to cultivate women's chastity as the highest national possession, for it is the only guarantee that we really are going to be the father of our children. . .This, and not masculine selfishness, is the reason why the law and morals make stricter demands on the woman than on the man with regard to premarital chastity and to marital fidelity.

Max Gruber,
German sex hygienist, 1920s

A woman's chastity consists, like an onion, of a series of coats.

Nathaniel Hawthorne

I loathe women who boast of their chastity, while secretly daring every sin.

Euripides

––––––

The only really indecent people are the chaste.

J.K. Huysmans

––––––

For the preservation of chastity, an empty and rumbling stomach and fevered lungs are indispensable.

Saint Jerome

––––––

Chastity enables the soul to breathe a pure air in the foulest places.

Joubert

––––––

Idleness is the ruin of chastity.

Latin proverb

––––––

If she seem not chaste to me
What care I how chaste she be?

Walter Raleigh

––––––

All women are chaste where there are no men.

Sanskrit proverb

Chastity is a monkish and evangelical superstition, a greater foe to natural temperance even than unintellectual sensuality; it strikes at the root of all domestic happiness, and consigns more than half of the human race to misery.

P.B. Shelley

I will find you twenty lascivious turtles ere one chaste man.

Shakespeare

Temperance is the nurse of chastity.

William Wycherley

Chauvinism, Male

The only position for women in SNCC (Student Non-Violent Coordinating Committee) is prone.

Stokely Carmichael

Women are only children of a larger growth.

Lord Chesterfield

A man of straw is worth more than a woman of gold.

John Florio

I tell you there isn't a thing under the sun that needs to be done at all, but what a man can do better than a woman, unless it's bearing children, and they do that in a poor make-shift way; it had better ha' been left to the men.

George Eliot

I am glad that I am not a man, as I should be obliged to marry a woman.

Anna Louise de Staël

For a man there are three certainties in life; death, taxes, and women. It is often difficult to say which is the worst.

Dr. Albert Ellis

I'm not primarily an entrepreneurial businessman, I'm primarily a playboy philosopher.

Hugh Hefner

Women were created for the comfort of men.

James Howell

I am very fond of the company of ladies; I like their beauty, I like their delicacy, I like their vivacity, and I like their silence.

Samuel Johnson

Men have broad and large chests, and small narrow hips, and more understanding than women, who have but small and narrow chests, and broad hips, to the end they should remain at home, sit still, keep house, and bear and bring up children.

Martin Luther

I want women to have all the faults and weaknesses they always had. I adore them, but we must keep them in their place. It's presumptuous for a woman to show me she is a doctor of mathematics. Comptometers can do that. What's more subtle and difficult is to know how to make a man feel important.

Marcello Mastroianni

Male chauvinism is. . .a shrewd method of extracting the maximum of work for the minimum of compensation.

Michael Korda

One can, to an almost laughable degree, infer what a man's wife is like from his opinions about women in general.

J.S. Mill

God created woman. And boredom did indeed cease from that moment—but many other things ceased as well. Woman was God's second mistake.

Friedrich Nietzsche

There's nothing so similar to one poodle dog as another poodle dog and that goes for women, too.

Pablo Picasso

There are only two kinds of women—goddesses and door-mats.

Pablo Picasso

A woman's place is in the bedroom and the kitchen, in that order.

Bobby Riggs

A woman's place. . .is in the bed or at the sink, and the extent of her travels should be from one to the other and back.

Caitlin Thomas

The woman is expressly formed to please the man.

Jean Jacques Rousseau

If all the harm that women have done
Were put in a bundle and rolled into one,
   Earth would not hold it,
   The sky could not enfold it,
It could not be lighted nor warmed by the sun.

J.K. Stephen

While I am not saying that there is a necessary connection between baboon patterns and human patterns. . .I am proposing that 'human nature' is such that it is 'unnatural' for females to engage in defense, police, and, by implication, high politics.

Lionel Tiger

To tell a woman what she may not do is to tell her what she can.

Spanish proverb

A woman is a solitary, helpless creature without a man.

Thomas Shadwell

Children

. . .the effort to inhibit all sex curiosity and pleasure in the child is quite useless; one succeeds only in creating repressions, obsessions, neuroses.

Simone de Beauvoir

(Try) to convince an eight-year-old that sexual intercourse is more fun than a chocolate ice cream cone.

Howard Gossage

Let not the fear of bad offspring deter you. . .You do your duty and the Holy One will do what pleases Him.

Hammuna

My obstetrician was so dumb that when I gave birth he forgot to cut the cord. For a year that kid followed me everywhere. It was like having a dog on a leash.

Joan Rivers

There are no instincts less harmful or more productive of delight in the whole range of human instinct and emotion than the desire for sex-love and the desire for children.

Dora Russell

I thought everybody in rock had illegitimate children.

Rod Stewart,
Rock musician

Knowing that children are healthfully curious—about sex as well as trucks and motors and planes—you can be active in helping them. . .Children want and need to learn a great deal; sex has a niche in this learning but it is not the whole show. . .One of the surprises is that sex barely holds its own with young children in competition with the million and one other ideas they also do not understand.

James L. Hymes, Jr.

Civilization

Society, when it rules "thumbs down" on extramarital relations, is guarding itself against destruction.
Mario A. Castallo

Our idea of sex wouldn't be recognizable to some other cultures though our range of choice is the widest ever. For a start it's over-genital: "sex" for our culture means putting the penis in the vagina.
Alex Comfort

Chastity is the cement of civilization and progress.
Mary Baker G. Eddy

The major civilizing force in the world is not religion, it's sex.
Hugh Hefner

A society in which women are taught anything but the management of a family, the care of men, and the creation of the future generation is a society which is on the way out.
L. Ron Hubbard

I believe that the sexual restraints devised by society are an unconscious manifestation of the wisdom of the human race. They deepen erotic power by controlling and focusing it, and the resulting energy is used to drive mankind upward along the path of civilization.

Norman Vincent Peale

I expect that woman will be the last thing civilized by man.

George Meredith

Custom controls the sexual impulse as it controls no other.

Margaret Sanger

Lots of sex for everybody, that's a solution to the world's problems.

R.E. (Ted) Turner

If there hadn't been women we'd still be squatting in a cave eating raw meat, because we made civilization in order to impress our girlfriends.

Orson Welles

Sex, to paraphrase Clausewitz, is the continuation of war by other means.

Ross Wetzsteon

Civilization has immensely elaborated the opportunities, the fruitfulness, and the significance of sex, and it also has increased the difficulties of achieving its ends.

Dr. Karl A. Menninger

Clothing

A dress that zips up the back will bring a husband and wife together.

James H. Boren

Women always show more taste in their choice of underclothing than in their choice of jewelry.

Chazal

When she raises her eyelids it's as if she were taking off all her clothes.

Colette

I dress for women—and I undress for men.

Angie Dickinson

What a man enjoys about a woman's clothes are his fantasies of how she would look without them.

Brendan Francis

Even the most respectable woman has a complete set of clothes in her wardrobe ready for a possible abduction.

> Sacha Guitry

───────

In silk and scarlet walks many a harlot.

> W.C. Hazlitt

───────

I think you can be contemporary without taking off your clothes.

> Sir Robert Helpman

───────

A skirt is no obstacle to extemporaneous sex, but it is physically impossible to make love to a girl while she is wearing trousers.

> Helen Lawrenson

───────

The robing and disrobing: that is the true traffic of love.

> Antonio Machado

───────

If you kept seeing Robert Redford stark naked on the screen, would he be a superstar today? No way. Or Gene Hackman showing everything? Their million dollar days would be over. I want to be in a movie where all the men take their clothes off and I don't.

> Cybill Shepherd

In the Seventies we shall move towards exposure and body cosmetics and certainly pubic hair, which we can now view on the cinema and stage, will become a fashion emphasis, although not necessarily blatant.

Mary Quant

Sex is a bad thing because it rumples the clothes.

Jackie Onassis

I'm just naturally respectful of pretty girls in tight-fitting sweaters.

Jack Parr

Brevity is the soul of lingerie.

Dorothy Parker

A dress has no meaning unless it makes a man want to take it off.

Françoise Sagan

The only method of creating sex appeal is by clothes. The woman of the 19th century was a masterpiece of sex appeal from the crown of her head to the soles of her feet. Everything about her except cheeks and nose was a secret.

George Bernard Shaw

If men were really what they profess to be they would not compel women to dress so that the facilities for vice would always be so easy.

Mary Edwards Walker

Women's clothes are painting and men's clothes are sculpture.

Barnett Newman

High heels were invented by a woman who had been kissed on the forehead.

Christopher Morley

Compatibility

It is the man and woman united that makes the complete human being. Separate, she wants his force of body and strength of reason; he, her softness, sensibility and acute discernment. Together, they are most likely to succeed in the world.

Benjamin Franklin

The sexes were made for each other, and only in the wise and loving union of the two is the fullness of health and duty and happiness to be expected.

William Hall

Grandeur and beauty come to the moment of sexual union from the total of what a man and a woman have been able to express in all the rest of their life together. Sexual union will then be the culmination of past love, and the sustenance of love to come.

Henri Gilbert

If you still behave in dancing rooms and other societies as I have seen you, I do not want to live—if you have done so, I wish this coming night may be my last. I cannot live without you, and not only you but chaste you; virtuous you.

John Keats

Eddie Fisher married to Elizabeth Taylor is like me trying to wash the Empire State Building with a bar of soap.

Don Rickles

Better to sit up all night, than to go to bed with a dragon.

Jeremy Taylor

Communication

Much polarity between men and women has centered around procreation. But the sex act itself is neither male nor female: it is a human being reaching out for the ultimate in communication with another human being.

Del Martin

A man is talking to you, nothing very personal. Look into his eyes as though tomorrow's daily double winners were there. Never let your eyes leave his. . . . This look has been referred to rather disdainfully as "hanging on his every word." It was good in your grandmother's day and it's still a powerhouse! (Is there any comparison between this and gazing all around the room to see if anybody good just came in?)

Helen Gurley Brown

What is truly indispensable for the conduct of life has been taught us by women—the small rules of courtesy; the actions that win us the warmth or deference of others; the words that assure us a welcome; the attitudes that must be varied to mesh with character or situation; all social strategy. It is listening to women that teaches us to speak to men.

Rémy de Gourmont

Oh, the years we waste and the tears we waste
And the work of our head and hand
Belong to the woman who did not know
(And now we know that she never could know)
And did not understand.

Rudyard Kipling

In any continuing relationship, any persistent feeling had better be expressed.

Carl Rogers

Competition

The law of battle for the possession of the female appears to prevail throughout the whole great class of mammals. Most naturalists will admit that the greater size, strength, courage, and pugnacity of the male, his special weapons of offence, as well as his special means of defence, have been acquired or modified through that form of selection which I have called sexual. This does not depend on any superiority in the general struggle for life, but on certain individuals of one sex, generally the males, being successful in conquering other males, and leaving a larger number of offspring to inherit their superiority than do the less successful males.

Charles Darwin

A girl should not expect special privileges because of her sex, but neither should she "adjust" to prejudice and discrimination. She must learn to compete. . .not as a woman, but as a human being.

Betty Friedan

Legitimate sex-competition brings out all that is best in man.
Charlotte Perkins Gilman

The competitive woman destroys something in a man. . .a thing called self-respect.

June Wilson

Conquest

Man's game for woman; fly where he will,
  Over clover, grass or stubble,
She'll wing you, feather you, or kill,
  Just as she takes the trouble.

Anonymous

The substance of our lives is woman. All other things are irrelevancies, hypocrisies, subterfuges. We sit talking of sports and politics, and all the while our hearts are filled with memories of women and the capture of women.

George Moore

It is one of the misfortunes of the professional Don Juan that his honor forbids him to refuse battle; he is in life like the Roman soldier upon duty, or like the sworn physician who must attend on all diseases.

R.L. Stevenson

Continence

Virtue has always been conceived of as victorious resistance to one's vital desire.

James Branch Cabell

Deliver yourself from the fetters of lust and passion. . .for God did not create you to be their captive, but that they should be your thralls, under your control, for the journey which is before you.

Al-Ghazali

Who is strong? The man who can control his passions.

Ben Zoma

You may say. . .we need not expect young men to live up to the ideal of continence. If so, I cannot agree. It is a duty we cannot shirk to point to the true ideal, to chastity, to a single standard of morals for men and women.

Josephus Daniels

Chastise your passions, that they may not chastise you.

Epictetus

A tranquil mind is health for the body; but passion is like rot in the bones.

Hebrew proverb

Continence is the only guarantee of an undefiled spirit, and the best protection against the promiscuity that cheapens and finally kills the power of love.

Gene Tunney

Present self-denial in order to gain greater benefits in the future is the hallmark of a rational human being.

Norman Vincent Peale

Men make a harness for their beasts; how much more should they fashion a harness for their passions.

Talmud

Contraception

Stop crime at its source! Support Planned Parenthood.

Robert Byrne

Whenever I hear people discussing birth control, I always remember that I was the fifth.

Clarence Darrow

You, as a person, never rate as bad, no matter how mistaken your sex acts. If you get women pregnant, your behavior certainly seems stupid and antisocial. But you cannot legitimately get labeled as hopelessly stupid or antisocial, since, as a result of this experience, you may change tomorrow and most scrupulously employ contraceptive techniques.

Albert Ellis

The command "be fruitful and multiply" (was) promulgated, according to our authorities, when the population of the world consisted of two persons.

William R. Inge

. . .he went on to remark gently that some women seemed to imagine birth control was a sort of magic; if they bought what was necessary and left it lying in a corner of a drawer, nothing more was needed. To this attitude of mind, he said, was due a number of births every year which would astound the public.

Doris Lessing

It is now quite lawful for a Catholic woman to avoid pregnancy by a resort to mathematics, though she is still forbidden to resort to physics or chemistry.

H.L. Mencken

What happened to the good old days of homemade ice cream and Trojans?. . .When did it become the woman's chore?

Gail Parent

Any use whatsoever of matrimony exercised in such a way that the act is deliberately frustrated in its natural power to generate life is an offense against the law of God and of nature, and those who indulge in such are branded with the guilt of a grave sin.

Pope Pius XI

A society which practices death control must at the same time practice birth control.

John Rock

If you cannot be chaste, be cautious.

Spanish proverb

Women who miscalculate are called "mothers."

Abigail Van Buren

Cultural Differences

Latins are tenderly enthusiastic. In Brazil they throw flowers at you. In Argentina they throw themselves.

Marlene Dietrich

Hollywood—out where the Sex begins.

Don Herold

As a result of the constraints of a hypocritical social morality, all men have become to some extent neurotic where sex is concerned.

Magnus Hirschfeld

In the Judeo-Christian culture, it seems to be that the sexual scenes are the biggest scenes in hell, scenes of things that are not to do, but in the Eastern religions, you find that the scenes are the things to do. In other words, the sexual things are the things that are good.

Doug Johns

The Japanese have a word for it. It's judo—the art of conquering by yielding. The Western equivalent of judo is, "Yes, dear."

J.P. McEvoy

Continental people have sex-lives.
The English have hot water bottles.

George Mikes

An attitude of sexuality is as pervasive in Cuba as the presence of Fidel Castro. You can feel sex in the atmosphere, on the street, in conversation, in people's actions. The Cubans seem to be thinking of it much of the time.

Sally Quinn

What used to be vices are becoming fashions.

Seneca

D

Death

Debauchery

Deception

Definitions or Descriptions

Deprivation

Desire

Differences, Behavioral

Differences, Physical

Discretion

Disinterest

Dislike

Divorce

Dominance

Drinking

Drive, Sex

Death

I am still of opinion that only two topics can be of the least interest to a serious and studious mood—sex and the dead.

William Butler Yeats

The difference between sex and death is, with death you can do it alone and nobody's going to make fun of you.

Woody Allen

There will be sex after death—we just won't be able to feel it.

Lily Tomlin

Debauchery

God has bidden us to refrain not only from other men's wives, but also from the common women of the town; when two bodies are joined together, He says, they are made into one. So the man who plunges into filth must of necessity with filthiness be stained.

Lactantius

Sex touches the heavens only when it simultaneously touches the gutter and the mud.

George Jean Nathan

I know your breed; all your fine officials debauch the young girls who are afraid to lose their jobs; that's as old as Washington.

Christina Stead

More than one woman has complained that all men want only one thing, and always the same.

Oswald Schwarz

Deception

Watch out for women's tricks!

Wolfgang A. Mozart

Woman is unspeakably more wicked than man, also cleverer. Goodness in woman is really nothing but a form of degeneracy.

Friedrich Nietzsche

Sex is politics.

Gore Vidal

Today the emphasis is on sex, and very little on the beauty of sexual relationship. Contemporary books and films portray it like a contest, which is absurd.

Henry Miller

———

'Twas ever thus with misses,
They leave the ancient home
To plant their Judas kisses
Upon some manly dome.

Anonymous

———

As Father Adam first was fool'd,
  A case that's still too common,
Here lies a man a woman rul'd:
  The Devil rul'd the woman.

Robert Burns

———

Believe a woman or an epitaph,
Or any other thing that's false.

George Gordon Byron

———

The woman whose behavior indicates that she will make a scene if she is told the truth asks to be deceived.

Elizabeth Jenkins

Then, my boy, beware of Daphne. Learn a
    lesson from a rat:
What is cunning in the kitten may be cruel
    in the cat.

R.U. Johnson

O woman, born first to believe us;
    Yea, also born first to forget;
Born first to betray and deceive us,
    Yet first to repent and regret!

Joaquin Miller

Definitions or Descriptions

Seriously, it is not so easy to define what the term sexual
includes. Everything connected with the differences between
the two sexes is perhaps the only way of hitting the mark; but
you will find that too general and indefinite.

Sigmund Freud

Anatomy is destiny.

Sigmund Freud

(Sex is) a fusion of many ideals into another's body.

Warren Goldberg

Sex, like all else between human beings, is never perfect.

Theodore Isaac Rubin

———

Bed is the poor man's opera.

Italian proverb

———

(Sex is) the metamorphosis of soul into body.

Warren Goldberg

———

I think sex is the greatest thing since Coca-Cola.

Cornelia Sharpe

Deprivation

. . . the total deprivation of it (sex) produces irritability.

Elizabeth Blackwell

———

What sex is, we don't know, but it must be some sort of fire. For it always communicates a sense of warmth, of glow. And when the glow becomes a pure shine, then we feel the sense of beauty.

D.H. Lawrence

Love can be as comforting as a deep bed, as exhilarating as champagne; it can be an ache, a joy, a yearning, a tenderness, or a destroying passion.

Derek & Julia Parker

Desire

Men are those creatures with two legs and eight hands.

Jane Mansfield

Give a man a free hand and he'll run it all over you.

Mae West

"Yes," I answered you last night;
  "No," this morning, sir, I say:
Colours seen by candle-light
  Will not look the same by day.

E.B. Browning

I have an intense desire to return to the womb. Anybody's.

Woody Allen

Love, as it is practiced in society, is merely the exchange of two momentary desires and the contact of two skins.

Nicolas Chamfort

What is it men in women do require?
The lineaments of gratified desire.
What is it women do in men require?
The lineaments of gratified desire.

William Blake

The man's desire is for the woman; but the woman's desire is
rarely other than for the desire of the man.

Coleridge

Desire pricks us daily. . .wherefore we must contrive to cir-
cumvent desire.

Lope de Vega

At a look, desire follows, with fulfilment close at heel.

Johann W. von Goethe

The question is not whether we have sex-desire, but whether
sex-desire has us.

E. Stanley Jones

. . . and then I asked him with my eyes to ask again yes and
then he asked me would I yes to say yes my mountain flower
and first I put my arms around him yes and drew him down to
me so he could feel my breasts all perfume yes and his heart
was going like mad and yes I said yes I will Yes.

James Joyce

The desire of a man for a woman is not directed at her because she is a human being, but because she is a woman. That she is a human being is of no concern to him.

Immanuel Kant

I think only of the joy and forget the folly—I lose sight of common sense, and follow my desire.

Arnaut de Mareuil

Lolita, light of my life, fire of my loins. My sin, my soul. Lo-lee-ta: the tip of the tongue taking a trip of three steps down the palate to tap, at three, on the teeth. Lo. Lee. Ta.

Vladimir Nabokov

We have two tyrannous physical passions: concupiscence and chastity. We become mad in pursuit of sex: we become equally mad in the persecution of that pursuit. Unless we gratify our desire the race is lost; unless we restrain it we destroy ourselves.

George Bernard Shaw

If men recognize no law superior to their desires, then they must fight when their desires collide.

R.H. Tawney

Women embrace their husbands without a particle of sex desire.

Dr. Mary Wood-Allen

Differences, Behavioral

Maidens' hearts are always soft; were that men's were truer!
William C. Bryant

Women cannot help moving and men cannot help being moved.

Anthony Burgess

Woman seems to differ from man in mental disposition, chiefly in her greater tenderness and less selfishness.
Charles Darwin

Man's conclusions are reached by toil. Woman arrives at the same by sympathy.

Ralph Waldo Emerson

The best man for a man and the best man for a woman are not the same.

Ortega Y Gasset

The woman possesses a theatrical exterior and a circumspect interior, while in the man it is the interior which is theatrical. The woman goes to the theater; the man carries it inside himself and is the impresario of his own life.

Ortega Y Gasset

Humanity is the virtue of a woman, generosity of a man. The fair sex, who have commonly much more tenderness than ours, have seldom so much generosity.

Adam Smith

Words are women, deeds are men.

George Herbert

Why can't a woman be more like a man?

Henry Higgins in
My Fair Lady (Lerner and Loewe)

Breathes there a man with soul so tough
Who says two sexes aren't enough?

Samuel Hoffenstein

Outdoors for man and dog; indoors for woman and cat.

Russian proverb

Ten measures of speech descended on the world; women took nine and men one.

Babylonian Talmud

In the long years liker must they grow;
The man be more of woman, she of man.

Alfred Lord Tennyson

As stolen love is pleasant to a man, so is it also to a woman; the man dissembles badly: she conceals desire more cleverly.

Ovid

———

Nobody will ever win the battle of the sexes. There's just too much fraternizing with the enemy.

Henry A. Kissinger

———

The female of the species is more deadly than the male.

Rudyard Kipling

———

If every woman in the world was weeping her heart out, men would be found dining, feeding, feasting.

A.W. Pinero

———

Love enters a man through his eyes; a woman, through her ears.

Polish proverb

———

Women in general want to be loved for what they are and men for what they accomplish.

Theodor Reik

———

Womankind lost equality in the Garden of Eden when Eve proved less trustworthy than Adam.

Ray Allen Riebel

. . . with women love usually proceeds from the soul to the senses and sometimes does not reach so far. . . with man it usually proceeds from the senses to the soul and sometimes never completes the journey.

Ellen Key

For men must work, and women must weep,
And the sooner it's over, the sooner to sleep.

Charles Kingsley

Women—they have to be nice-looking. But men—they must be smart.

Ivana Trump

Men and women are quite different in temperament and needs, and the feminists efforts to deny this is increasing the rivalry between the sexes and impairing the pleasure of both.

Benjamin Spock

All women become like their mothers. That is their tragedy. No man does. That is his.

Oscar Wilde

Differences, Physical

I love men, not because they are men, but because they are not women.

Christina, Queen of Sweden

A woman's head is usually over ears in her heart. Man seems to have been designed for the superior being of the two; but as things are, I think women are generally better creatures than men. They have, taken universally, weaker appetites and weaker intellects, but they have much stronger affections. A man with a bad heart has been sometimes saved by a strong head; but a corrupt woman is loft for ever.

S.T. Coleridge

There is more difference within the sexes than between them.

Ivey Compton-Burnett

Man begins by making love and ends by loving a woman; woman begins by loving a man and ends by loving love.

Rémy de Gourmont

. . . the first sexual stirrings of little girls, so masked, so complex, so foolish as compared with the sex of little boys.

Lillian Hellman

All too many men still seem to believe, in a rather naive and egocentric way, that what feels good to them is automatically what feels good to women.

Shere Hite

For contemplation he and valor formed,
For softness she, and sweet attractive grace.

John Milton

Women are quite unlike men. Women have higher voices, longer hair, smaller waistlines, daintier feet and prettier hands. They also invariably have the upper hand.

Stephen Potter

But for her sex, a woman is a man; she has the same organs, the same needs, the same faculties. The machine is the same in its construction; its parts, its working, and its appearance are similar. Regard it as you will, the difference is only in degree.

Jean Jacques Rousseau

Men, at most differ as Heaven and earth,
But women, worst and best, as Heaven and Hell.

Alfred Lord Tennyson

I would rather go to bed with Lillian Russell stark naked than Ulysses S. Grant in full military regalia.

Mark Twain

Nothing is either all masculine or all feminine except having sex.

Marlo Thomas

Except for their genitals, I don't know what immutable differences exist between men and women.

Naomi Weisstein

Discretion

Women do not transgress the bounds of decorum so often as men, but when they do they go greater lengths. For with reason somewhat weaker, they have to contend with passions somewhat stronger; besides, a female by one transgression forfeits her place in society forever; if once she fails, it is the fall of Lucifer.

C.C. Colton

As a jewel of Gold in a swine's snout, so is a fair woman which is without discretion.

Proverbs

Disinterest

I should say that the majority of women (happily for society) are not much troubled with sexual feeling of any kind.

William Action

Sex may be a hallowing and renewing experience, but more often it will be distracting, coercive, playful, frivolous, discouraging, dutiful and even boring.

Leslie H. Farber

Do not wonder at the man who runs after a heartless coquette, but keep your wonder for the man who does not.

George Groddeck

One thing I've learned in all these years is not to make love when you really don't feel it; there's probably nothing worse you can do to yourself than that.

Norman Mailer

I married the world—the world is my husband. That is why I'm so young. No sex. Sex is the most tiring thing in the world.

Elsa Maxwell

I don't know whether you've ever had a woman eat an apple while you were doing it. . . . Well you can imagine how that affects you.

Henry Miller

=======

As far as I am concerned being any gender is a drag.

Patti Smith

=======

After being alive, the next hardest work is sex . . . Some people get energy from sex and some people lose energy from sex. I have found that it's too much work. But if you have the time for it, and you need the exercise—then you should do it.

Andy Warhol

=======

All this fuss about sleeping together. For physical pleasure I'd sooner go to my dentist any day.

Evelyn Waugh

Dislike

He wondered why sexual shyness, which excites the desire of dissolute women, arouses the contempt of decent ones.

Colette

Making love as if it were something one could make, as if it were making do or making believe. Hating her own hands, hating the thin desperate clinging body that responded by heart to echoes of old movements, like a mechanical toy. . . . Its working was an unbearable affront; it accused her. It made her admit the truth. I don't care if it still works, I hate it—I don't want it any more.

Lois Gould

I have never hated a man enough to give his diamonds back.

Zsa Zsa Gabor

I can live without it all—love with its blood pump, sex with its messy hungers, men with their peacock strutting, their silly sexual baggage, their wet tongue in my ear and their words like little sugar suckers with sour centers.

Erica Jong

We have no right to boast of despising and combating carnal pleasure, if we cannot feel it, if we know nothing of it, of its charms and power, and its most alluring beauties. I know both, and so have a right to speak.

Michel de Montaigne

Sex as an institution, sex as a general notion, sex as a problem, sex as a platitude—all this is something I find too tedious for words. Let us skip sex.

Vladimir Nabokov

For some years she had been thinking she was not much inclined towards sex. . . . It is not merely a lack of pleasure in sex, it is dislike of the excitement. And it is not merely dislike, it is worse, it is boredom.

Murial Spark

On the brink of being satiated, desire still appears infinite.

Jean Rostand

Sex to me is a beautiful thing and shouldn't be abused. You should't sleep with just anybody, you shouldn't sleep with anybody for money, you should sleep with somebody you really like and that's it. And it's not a power or control thing. That's what I don't like about sex. That's why I haven't slept with anyone for two years.

Poly Styrene

Sex is the biggest nothing of all time.

Andy Warhol

Divorce

Your acquaintance, D. Rodrigue, has had a small accident befallen him. Mr. Annesley found him in bed with his wife, prosecuted, and brought a bill of divorce into Parliament. Those things grow more fashionable every day.

Mary Wortley Montagu

I see no marriages which sooner fail than those contracted on account of beauty and amorous desire.

Michel de Montaigne

Each day they decide to divorce, but each night they head for bed.

Hebrew proverb

Divorce is the sacrament of adultery.

French proverb

Did you hear about the fellow who blamed arithmetic for his divorce? His wife put two and two together?

Earl Wilson

Dominance

The best of all possible marriages is a seesaw in which first one, then the other partner is dominant.

Joyce Brothers

A strong man doesn't have to be dominant toward a woman. He doesn't match his strength against a woman weak with love for him. He matches it against the world.

Marilyn Monroe

Male domination has had some very unfortunate effects. It has made the most intimate of human relations, that of marriage, one of master and slave, instead of one between equal partners.

Bertrand Russell

I always run into strong women who are looking for weak men to dominate them.

Andy Warhol

Drinking

Don't be fooled into believing alcohol is an effective turn-on. A moderate amount reduces the inhibitions—but as Shakespeare said, it increases the desire but damages the performance.

Henry W. Brosin

There never was a drunken woman, or a woman who loved strong drink, who was chaste, if the opportunity of being the contrary presented itself to her.

William Cobbett

One more drink and I'll be under the host.

Dorothy Parker

Drive, Sex

Sex drive: A physical craving that begins in adolescence and ends at marriage.

Robert Byrne

The sexual drive is nothing but the motor memory of previously experienced pleasure.

Wilhelm Reich

Any relationship whose survival demands that you or your partner play a rigidly defined role and suppress natural traits is not a healthy union.

Adrian Warren

E

Embarrassment
Emotions
Enjoyment
Equality
Experience
Exploitation

Embarrassment

She blushed like a well-trained sunrise.

Margaret Halsey

Anthea made me tie her shoe;
I did, and kissed the instep too;
And would have kissed unto her knee,
Had not her blush rebuked me.

Robert Herrick

If the bed could tell all it knows it would put many to the blush.

John Ray

Emotions

A woman's desire for revenge outlasts all her other emotions.

Cyril Connolly

Heav'n has no rage like love to hatred turn'd,
Nor hell a fury like a woman scorn'd.

Congreve

After the relationship has ended: Feel what you are feeling. Mourn. Take time to think about yourself. Denying what you feel doesn't work. Figure out what you have learned by being in this relationship. Only then will you be free to move on.

Elaine Hatfield

It is because of men that women dislike each other.

Jean de La Bruyère

So long as the emotional feelings between the couple are right, so long as there is mutual trust and love, their bodies will invariably make the appropriate responses.

David R. Mace

To my embarrassment I was born in bed with a lady.

Wilson Mizner

I did not sleep, I never do when I am over-happy, over-unhappy, or in bed with a strange man.

Edna O'Brien

It's hard to be growing up in this climate where sex at its most crude and cold is O.K. but feeling is somehow indecent.

May Sarton

Love is an infusion of intense feeling, a fine madness that makes you drunk, and when one is in love, life can be a succession of freefalls while working without a net.

Merle Shain

You should make a woman angry if you wish her to love.

Publilius Syrus

The best book for two people to read to improve their love life together is the chronicle of each other's feelings about themselves.

David Viscott

Enjoyment

The fact of human experience seems to be that persons enjoy deeper, more lasting, and more profound satisfaction when normal experience of sex lust is not primarily an end in itself but a symbolic expression of other values.

Peter A. Bertocci

Sex is the most fun you can have without smiling.

Anonymous

Women are a problem, but if you haven't already guessed, they're the kind of problem I enjoy wrestling with.

Warren Beatty

It can be great fun to have an affair with a bitch.

Louis Auchincloss

I love the sex, and sometimes would reverse
  The tyrant's wish that mankind only had
One neck, which he with one fell stroke might pierce.
My wish is quite as wide, but not so bad. . .
That womankind had but one rosy mouth,
To kiss them all at once from North to South.

George Gordon Byron

Sex ought to be a wholly satisfying link between two affectionate people from which they emerge unanxious, rewarded, and ready for more.

Alex Comfort

The whole joy of sex-with-love is that there are no rules, so long as you enjoy, and the choice is practically unlimited.

Alex Comfort

Sunday would be abolished—except between consenting adults in private.

Penelope Gilliatt

What good is it to reap immediate pleasure?
The joy's not near so great, I say,
As if you first prepare the ground
With every sort of idle folly,
Knead and make ready your pretty dolly,
As many Romance tales expound.
                              Johann W. von Goethe

I love men like some people like good food or wine.
                              Germaine Greer

I only like two kinds of men; domestic and foreign.
                              Mae West

Too much of a good thing can be wonderful.
                              Mae West

Girls who are having a good sex thing stay in New York. The
rest want to spend their summer vacations in Europe.
                              Gail Parent

I'd much rather be having fun in the bedroom instead of
doing all this talking in the living room.
                              Elizabeth Ray

In all enjoyment there is a choice between enjoying the other and enjoying yourself through the instrumentality of the other. The first is the enjoyment of love, the second is the enjoyment of lust. When people enjoy themselves through each other, that is merely mutual lust.

John MacMurray

Equality

I refuse to consign the whole male sex to the nursery. I insist on believing that some men are my equals.

Brigid Brophy

I'm all for women having equal rights. But I repeat, women shouldn't fight bulls because a bullfighter is and should be a man.

Paco Camino

There is no equality except in a cemetery. There are differences in physical structure and biological function. . . There is more difference between male and female than between a horse chestnut and a chestnut horse.

Emmanuel Celler

You're used. Used by what you are, eat, believe and who you sleep with. You can stop it. If you want equality, it has to start in bed. If he won't give it to you there, rip him off.

Jane Gallion

—————

A woman's feeling for a man inferior to herself is pity rather than love.

Anna Louise de Staël

—————

Give a woman a job and she grows balls.

Jack Gelber

—————

The only jobs for which no man is qualified are human incubator and wet nurse. Likewise, the only job for which no woman is or can be qualified is sperm donor.

Wilma Scott Heide

—————

Men seldom make passes at a girl who surpasses.

Franklin P. Jones

—————

If women are expected to do the same work as men, we must teach them the same things.

Plato

—————

No man is a match for a woman till he's married.

R.S. Surtees

Sex pervades all nature, yet the male and female tree and vine and shrub rejoice in the same sunshine and shade. The earth and air are free to all the fruits and flowers, yet each absorbs what best ensures its growth.

Elizabeth Cady Stanton

There are really not many jobs that actually require a penis or a vagina, and all other occupations should be open to everyone.

Gloria Steinem

The little rift between the sexes is astonishingly widened by simply teaching one set of catchwords to the girls and another to the boys.

Robert Louis Stevenson

Experience

When the girl you kiss gives as good as you give, you are not getting firsts.

Anonymous

It's the good girls who keep the diaries; the bad girls never have had the time.

Tallulah Bankhead

The proof that experience teaches us nothing is that the end of one love does not prevent us from beginning another.

Paul Bourget

Boast not thyself to know women, for thou knowest not what the next damsel shall teach thee.

Gelett Burgess

First I lost my weight, then I lost my voice, and now I lost Onassis.

Maria Callas

The kind of knowledge that is picked up through illicit relations is likely to have to be unlearned.

Louise Fox Connell

The sexual embrace can only be compared with music and with prayer.

Havelock Ellis

With all her experience, every woman expects to do better when she marries a second time, and some do.

Leonard Feather

Males have made asses of themselves writing about female sexual experience.

William Howell Masters

The first girl you go to bed with is always pretty.

Walter Matthau

There is an inverse relationship between the number of how-to-do-it books perused by a person, or rolling off the presses in a society, and the amount of sexual passion or even pleasure experienced by the persons involved.

Rollo May

Between two evils, I always pick the one I never tried before.

Mae West

The Book of Life begins with a man and a woman in a garden. It ends with Revelation.

Oscar Wilde

Exploitation

If I'd played ball with the producers in Hollywood I could have made it long ago as an actress. But I couldn't. Someone like Grace Kelly came along looking every inch a lady, and they'd give her a chance to act. Producers wouldn't attack her. But me! As soon as I walked in they started chasing me around the desks.

Linda Christian

I should like to know what is the proper function of women, if it is not to make reasons for husbands to stay at home, and still stronger reasons for bachelors to go out.

George Eliot

Instead of hustling for sex, we'll be hustling for the Lord.

Larry Flynt

The female segregated to the uses of sex alone naturally deteriorates in racial development.

Charlotte Perkins Gilman

Indeed, Hugh Hefner is beginning to seem more and more like everyone's kindly and slightly bewildered uncle.

Bob Greene

Honey, whatever women do, they do best after dark.

John Lindsay

Having fought for the 1st amendment before Penthouse was born I wish (the first amendment) was in better hands than a magazine that specializes in close-ups of women's orifices.

Louis Nizer
(Attorney for Rancho La Costa in its $630 million libel suit against Penthouse Magazine).

===

A sex symbol becomes a thing. I hate being a thing.

Marilyn Monroe

===

Politics is sex in a hula-hoop.

Richard Reeves

===

The sex symbol always remains, but the sophisticated woman has become old hat.

Rosalind Russell

===

A woman reading Playboy feels a little like a Jew reading a Nazi manual.

Gloria Steinem

===

There are three things men can do with women: love them, suffer for them, or turn them into literature.

Stephen Stills

F

Face
Faking Orgasm
Fantasies
Fear
Fidelity
Flattery
Flirtation
Food
Foolishness
Freedom, Sexual
Friendship
Frigidity

Face

An ugly face is the only effective guardian of a woman's virtue.

Immanuel of Rome

A woman, the more curious she is about her face, is commonly the more careless about her house.

Ben Jonson

Men seldom make passes
At girls who wear glasses.

Dorothy Parker

Faking Orgasm

. . .he wondered again, how much of her desire was passion and how much grasping: girls used sex to get a hold on you, he knew—it was so easy for them to pretend to be excited.

Sallie Bingham

My dear I'm never off duty except when I'm in bed—and not always then.

Dorita Fairlie Bruce

A man can feel kinship with the gods if his wife can make him believe he can cause a flowering within her. If she doesn't feel it she must bend every effort to pretend. This is the worthiest duplicity on earth; I heartily recommend it to discontented wives.

Marion Hilliard

Really, I pity the girl whose place, let us say, cannot give her
    Pleasure it gives to the man, pleasure she ought to enjoy.
So, if you have to pretend, be sure the pretense is effective,
    Do your best to convince, prove it by rolling your eyes,
Prove by your motions, your moans, your sighs, what a
        pleasure it gives you.
    Ah, what a shame! That part has its own intimate signs.

Ovid

Fantasies

When turkeys mate they think of swans.

Johnny Carson

Last time I tried to make love to my wife nothing was happening, so I said to her, "What's the matter, you can't think of anybody either?"

Rodney Dangerfield

An improper mind is a perpetual feast.

Logan Pearsall Smith

Nine-tenths of that which is attributed to sexuality is the work of our magnificent ability to imagine, which is no longer an instinct, but exactly the opposite: a creation.

Ortega Y Gasset

When you're extremely sensually attracted to someone, then you go to bed with him, you've fulfilled the sexual fantasy and some of the excitement is gone. Then you start to look at his personality more closely.

Susie Scott,
Playboy Playmate, May, 1983

Fear

Free love is seldom free. Teens pay for it in worry—the fear that they'll get caught, or that their partner may tire of them. It's hurried and furtive and not much fun.

Helen Bottel

Take off your shell along with your clothes.

Alex Comfort

Who bathes in worldly joys, swims in a world of fears.

Phineas Fletcher

A man is always afraid of a woman who loves him too well.

John Gay

When you're living with someone it's fantastic. Everything that he does you do. They're so frightened of losing you they've got to keep you satisfied all the time.

Nell Dunn

He went to Europe as a boy, where in Geneva his father arranged for a prostitute. He was so terrified by the experience that he didn't marry until he was 67 years old.

John Leonard of Borges

In our civilization, men are afraid that they will not be men enough and women are afraid that they might be considered only women.

Theodor Reik

Men are not given awards and promotions for bravery in intimacy.

Gail Sheehy

Fidelity

Christ says, don't consider yourself better than someone else because one guy screws a whole bunch of women, while the other guy is loyal to his wife.

Jimmy Carter

He who wins a thousand common hearts is entitled to some renown; but he who keeps undisputed sway over the heart of a coquette is indeed a hero.

Washington Irving

It is natural
For a woman to be wild with her husband when he
Goes in for secret love.

Euripides

Between a man and his wife a husband's infidelity is nothing. The man imposes no bastards on his wife.

Samuel Johnson

A man will take any girl to bed, and it has nothing to do with any attraction for her or his love for his wife. A woman may like to think she is the same, that she is equal, but she's not, because when she loves her man, she'll be faithful to him. A woman's love for a man is greater than a man's love for a woman.

Tom Jones

Though she does not pique herself upon fidelity to any one man (which is but a narrow way of thinking), she boasts that she has always been true to her nation, and, notwithstanding foreign attacks, has always reserved her charms for the use of her own countrymen.

Mary Wortley Montagu

They are foes of mutual fidelity who teach that the ideas prevailing at the present time concerning false and harmful relations with a third party can be tolerated, and that a greater freedom of feeling and action should be permitted to man or wife.

Pope Pius XI

One man's folly is another man's wife.

Helen Rowland

I should not regard physical infidelity as a very grave cause and should teach people that it is to be expected and tolerated.

Bertrand Russell

No man worth having is true to his wife, or can be true to his wife, or ever was or ever will be.

John Vanbrugh

Save a boyfriend for a rainy day, and another in case it doesn't rain.

Mae West

Young men want to be faithful and are not;
Old men want to be faithless and cannot.

Oscar Wilde

Let him who wantonly sports away the peace of a poor lady consider what discord he sows in families; how often he wrings the heart of a hoary parent; how often he rouses the fury of a jealous husband; how he extorts from the abused woman curses poured out in the bitterness of her soul.

Richard Steele

I have no doubt that a sensitive woman may come to the point of feeling no physical pleasure but with the man she loves. It's the opposite with the savage.

Stendhal

Those who are faithful know only the trivial side of love; it is the faithless who know love's tragedies.

Oscar Wilde

Marriages are like diets. They can be ruined by having a little dish on the side.

Earl Wilson

Flattery

A Total Woman caters to her man's special quirks, whether it be in salads, sex, or sports.

Marabel Morgan

It is the male that gives charms to womankind, that produces an air in their faces, a grace in their motions, a softness in their voices, and a delicacy in their complexions.

Joseph Addison

There's a difference between beauty and charm. A beautiful woman is one I notice. A charming woman is one who notices me.

John Erskine

When you see a woman who can go nowhere without a staff of admirers, it is not so much because they think she is beautiful, it is because she has told them they are handsome.

Jean Giraudoux

Be cautious in listening to the addresses of men. Art thou pleased with smiles and flattering words? Remember that man often smiles and flatters most when he would betray thee.

Noah Webster

If she think not well of me,
What care I how fair she be?

George Wither

Flirtation

Life is not long enough for a coquette to play all her tricks in.

Joseph Addison

A maid that laughs is half taken.

English proverb

No man does right by a woman at a party.

Harry Golden

Flirtation is at the bottom of woman's nature, although all do not practice it, some being restrained by fear, others by sense.

La Rochefoucauld

The art of flirtation is dying. A man and woman are either in love these days or just friends. In the realm of love, reticence and sophistication should go hand in hand, for one of the joys of life is discovery.

Marya Mannes

Flirtation—attention without intention.

Max O'Neil

In part to blame is she which hath without consent been only
    tried:
He comes too near that comes to be denied.

Thomas Overbury

Food

Anyone who eats three meals a day should understand why
cookbooks outsell sex books three to one.

L.M. Boyd

Eat plenty of garlic. This guarantees you twelve hours of
sleep—alone—every night, and there's nothing like rest to
give you shining orbs.

Chris Chase

Great food is like great sex—the more you have the more you
want.

Gail Greene

Eating after lovemaking may even be a way of reestablishing
order—by doing so, you are returning to a "normal" activity,
one that makes you feel in control again after being swept
away by sexual passion.

Maj-Britt Rosenbaum

Foolishness

I'm not denyin' the women are foolish: God Almighty made 'em to match the men.

George Eliot

Man's shame is between his legs, a fool's between his cheeks.

Moses IBN Ezra

The ass is the face of the soul of sex.

Charles Bukowski

Beauty and folly are generally companions.

Baltasar Gracian

My only books
Were woman's looks,
And folly's all they taught me.

Thomas Moore

Whenever at a party, I have been in the mood to study fools, I have always looked for a great beauty: they always gather round her like flies around a fruit-stall.

Jean Paul Richter

I think any man in business would be foolish to fool around with his secretary. If it's somebody else's secretary, fine!
Barry Goldwater

Freedom, Sexual

Free love is sometimes love but never freedom.
Elizabeth Bibesco

When the sexual energy of the people is liberated they will break the chains.
Julian Beck

In the U.S.S.R. . . .since private property and capital have been abolished, love is free of all. . .material considerations, and adultery no longer exists.
A Soviet sociologist

No one can be perfectly free till all are free; no one can be perfectly moral till all are moral; no one can be perfectly happy till all are happy.
Herbert Spencer

Women are more willingly and more gloriously chaste when they are least restrained of their liberty.
John Webster

Friendship

A man and a woman make far better friendships than can exist between two of the same sex; but with this condition, that they never have made, or are to make, love with each other.

George Gordon Byron

Wherever you go, have a woman friend.

Irish proverb

Most of the time, a friendship lasts a lot longer than love.

Marlene Janssen,
Playboy Playmate, Nov. 1982.

A woman may very well form a friendship with a man, but for this to endure, it must be assisted by a little physical antipathy.

Friedrich Nietzsche

No woman ever hates a man for being in love with her, but many a woman hates a man for being a friend to her.

Alexander Pope

Platonic love is love from the neck up.

Thyra Samter Winslow

Frigidity

Frigidity is the word used to describe impaired sexual feeling in women. . .and was probably coined by a man.

David M. Reuben

Men always fall for frigid women because they put on the best show.

Fanny Brice

I hate a woman who offers herself because she ought to do so, and, cold and dry, thinks of her sewing when she's making love.

Ovid

G

Game-playing
Giving
Group Sex
Guilt

Game-playing

Love is a sport in which the hunter must contrive to have the quarry in pursuit.

Jean Kerr

To win a woman in the first place one must please her, then undress her, and then somehow get her clothes back on her. Finally, so that she will allow you to leave her, you've got to annoy her.

Jean Giraudoux

Women can always be caught: that's the first rule of the game.

Ovid

The soul has become a department of sex, and sex has become a department of politics.

Octavio Paz

I could hear the lovely, tiny swallowing gulps—you cover all ages in the sex-play cycle, from nursing infant to death in one terrifying swoop of the sexual plot.

Jill Robinson

Giving

What they (women) like to give, they love to be robbed of.

Ovid

We must know how to give sexuality the high and exact place that belongs to it when it serves to express the gesture of an open-handed giver and not the grasping move of a selfish hoarder.

Henri Gilbert

Now there is no nobility in a man who can receive pleasure where he gives none; it is a mean soul that is willing to owe everything and takes pleasure in fostering relations with persons to whom he is a burden.

Michel de Montaigne

Woman gives herself as a prize to the weak and as a prop to the strong, and no man ever has what he should.

Pavese

Ever since Eve gave Adam the apple, there has been a misunderstanding between the sexes about gifts.

Nan Robertson

Group Sex

Sex is nobody's business except the three people involved.

Anonymous

If you swing both ways, you really swing. I just figure, you know, double your pleasure.

Joan Baez

If God had meant for us to have group sex, He'd have given us more organs.

Malcolm Bradbury

No bed is big enough to hold three.

German proverb

If you don't swing, don't ring.

Sign, front door of
Playboy Mansion

Group sex could jeopardize a relationship and it could enhance it—Again, it all depends on your attitude. If a woman is very jealous, then she'd better not engage in group sex. Or perhaps she'd better, in order to work on her jealousy.

Shirley Zussman

Guilt

When lovely woman stoops to folly,
  And finds too late that men betray,
What charm can soothe her melancholy?
  What art can wash her guilt away?

Oliver Goldsmith

She was the type that would wake up in the morning and immediately start apologizing.

Woody Allen

One man's remorse is another man's reminiscence.

Gerald Horton Bath

Young people are moving away from feeling guilty about sleeping with somebody to feeling guilty if they are not sleeping with someone.

Margaret Mead

The follies which a man regrets most in his life are those which he didn't commit when he had the opportunity.

Helen Rowland

When grown-ups do it it's kind of dirty—that's because there's no one to punish them.

Tuesday Weld

H

Happiness
Homosexuality
Homosexuals
Humor

Happiness

I was never worried about any sex investigation in Washington. All the men on my staff can type.

Bella Abzug

If the heart of a man is depress'd with cares,
The mist is dispell'd when a woman appears.

John Gay

Time has no importance. The most remarkable thing is that the other person's happiness becomes at least as important as your own. A person who loves you wants you to be happy forever.

Allan Martin Kaufman

All this talk about sex, all this worry about sex—big deal. The sun makes me happy. I eat a good fish, he makes me happy. I sleep with a good man, he makes me happy.

Melina Mercouri

The sexual organs are simply the means of exchanging sexual sensations. The real business is transacted at the emotional level. Thus, the foundation for sexual happiness—or misery— is laid not in the bedroom but at the breakfast table.

David R. Reuben

I'll match my flops with anybody's but I wouldn't have missed 'em. Flops are a part of life's menu and I've never been a girl to miss out on any of the courses.

Rosalind Russell

The person is in search of the absolute, i.e., perfect happiness. To use sex as a substitute for the absolute is a vain attempt to turn the copy into the original.

Fulton J. Sheen

I am very tender-hearted on love-cases, especially to women, whose happiness does really depend, for some time at least, on the accomplishment of their wishes: they cannot conceive that another swain might be just as charming. I am not so indulgent to men, who do know that one romance is as good as another.

Horace Walpole

Homosexuality

In my first dream I was a Judge who was judging a young man who hadn't been very wise in his behaviour with a Boy Scout. This was my summing up: 'You are completely innocent and you leave this court without a stain on your character; but don't do it again; and I advise you in future to employ girl guides.'

Christabel Aberconway

Homosexuality is funny, provided it's on the telly; off the telly homosexuals are only fit for being punched up.

Philip Adams

====

God says that someone who practices homosexuality shall not inherit the Kingdom of God. God is very plain on that.

Anita Bryant

====

I cannot sit in judgment of anyone. I have been forgiven a great deal myself. But there are some things that God just does not condone—and homosexuality is just one of them. It says so many times in the Bible.

Dale Evans

====

To the heterosexual man, who is secure in his own feelings of sexuality, the homosexual, whether male or female, offers no more threat than a flower in bloom. He welcomes all sexuality that is in blossom.

Brendan Francis

====

Homosexuality would certainly be an easier subject to describe and to analyze if it were confined to the people who practice it.

Brendan Francis

====

There's nothing wrong with going to bed with somebody of your own sex. . . People should be very free with sex—they should draw the line at goats.

Elton John

Homosexuality has always existed, of course, but only recently has it been openly talked about. With this new openness, many myths about homosexuality are being dispelled. One is that a homosexual cannot be a useful, happy, productive person. Many committed homosexuals are. . . Disappearing, too, is the idea that an individual who has engaged in homosexual practices cannot lead a normal, heterosexual life. He can—if he wants to.

Lawrence J. Hatterer

If the need for affection is concentrated on the same sex, this may be one of the determining factors in latent or manifest homosexuality. The need for affection may be directed toward the same sex if the way to the other sex is barred by too much anxiety.

Karen Horney

The whole idea of homosexual experience in a man's life is so much more written about, only because women's homosexuality isn't taken seriously. Even when they do think about it, men think a woman homosexual could be turned around by a good night in bed with a man. It's not threatening, because they assume there couldn't be true love between two women.

Gloria Steinem

There is probably no sensitive heterosexual alive who is not preoccupied with his latent homosexuality.

Norman Mailer

It's easier to be accepted in our society as a murderer than as a homosexual.

Abby Mann

If God dislikes gays so much, how come he picked Michelangelo, a known homosexual, to paint the Sistine Chapel ceiling while assigning Anita (Bryant) to go on TV and push orange juice?

Mike Royko

'Gay' used to be one of the most agreeable words in the language. Its appropriation by a notably morose group is an act of piracy.

Arthur Schlesinger, Jr.

I guess they're entitled to remain as sick as they like as long as they like (commenting on homosexuals).

Samuel Ichiye Hayakawa

Homosexuals

I think you (Noel Coward) are wonderful and charming, and if I should ever change from liking girls better, you would be my first thought.

Humphrey Bogart

I love gay people. . . But they are not a minority whose rights have to be protected. They are not like blacks, because black sticks. . . If gays are granted rights, next we'll have to give rights to prostitutes and to people who sleep with Saint Bernards and to nail-biters.

Anita Bryant

If God had meant to have homosexuals, he would have created Adam and Bruce.

Anita Bryant

I say I'm a homosexual who has had heterosexual experiences.

Truman Capote

I am the last of Britain's stately homos.

Quentin Crisp

Homosexuals have time for everybody. . .every detail of lives of real people, however mundane it may be, seems romantic to them.

Quentin Crisp

Gentlemen don't prefer blondes. If I were writing that book today, I'd call it 'Gentlemen Prefer Gentlemen.'

Anita Loos

They gave me a medal for killing two men and discharged me for loving one.

Leonard P. Matlovich

Human relations are possible between homosexuals just as between a man and a woman. Homosexuals can love, give, elevate others and elevate themselves. It's surely better to get into bed with a boy friend than to go traveling in Nazi Germany when France has been defeated and strangled.

Jean-Paul Sartre

Homosexuals as well as heterosexuals have emotional hang-ups. Though that usually comes to an abrupt end—when the boy asks for more money.

Gore Vidal

Homosexuals make the best friends because they care about you as a woman and are not jealous. They love you but don't try to screw up your head.

Bianca Jagger

Humor

The time will come—it's a great way off—when a joke about sex will be not so much objectionable as unintelligible. . . . To the perfectly enfranchised mind it should be as impossible to joke about sex as about mind or digestion or physiology.
W. N. P. Barbellion

Sex is like having dinner: sometimes you joke about the dishes, sometimes you take the meal seriously.
Woody Allen

Humor is like sex. Those who do it don't talk about it.
Marty Feldman

If you can make a woman laugh you can do anything with her.
Nicol Williamson

I

Importance
Intelligence
Intercourse

Importance

The omnipresent process of sex, as it is woven into the whole texture of our man's or woman's body, is the pattern of all the process of our life.

Havelock Ellis

Man cannot live by bed alone.

Anonymous

Life begins at the centerfold and expands outward.

Lisa Baker

Nothing is potent against love save impotence.

Samuel Butler

Physiological expenditure is a superficial way of self expression. People who incline towards physical love accomplish nothing at all.

Salvador Dali

Sex is about as important as a cheese sandwich. But a cheese sandwich, if you ain't got one to put in your belly, is extremely important.

Ian Dury

Perhaps it is just a hangover from the past, but even those writers who declare that the importance of sex is its sheer pleasure do so with an evangelical zeal that is directive rather than permissive.

Elizabeth Janeway

(Sex is) something popular because it's centrally located.

Shannon Carse

A single night of universal love could save everything.

Roland Giguere

Sex. . .is the beat of the universe.

Maurice Girodias

(Sex is) a sport, a recreation, a pastime.

Aldous Huxley

Sex is one of the nine reasons for reincarnation. . .The other eight are unimportant.

Henry Miller

Sex is the cure-all.

Joe Namath

Civilized people cannot fully satisfy their sexual instinct without love.

Bertrand Russell

Sex. . .is a subject like any other subject. Every bit as interesting as agriculture.

Muriel Spark

———

Sex, treated properly, can be one of the most gorgeous things in the world.

Elizabeth Taylor

———

Sex is important, but by no means the only important thing in life.

Mary Whitehouse

———

Freud found sex an outcast in the outhouse, and left it in the living room an honored guest.

W. Beran Wolfe

Intelligence

Better that a girl has beauty than brains because boys see better than they think.

Anonymous

———

I am constantly amazed when I talk to young people to learn how much they know about sex and how little about soap.

Billie Burke

———

Women trade with the weaknesses and follies of men, not with their reason.

Nicolas Chamfort

In contrast to the concentric structure of the feminine mind, there are always epicenters in that of the man. The more masculine, in a spiritual sense, a man is, the more his mind is disjointed in separate compartments.

Ortega Y Gasset

―――

Can you recall a woman who ever showed you with pride her library?

De Casseres

―――

There is no female mind. The brain is not an organ of sex. As well speak of a female liver.

Charlotte Perkins Gilman

―――

Generally speaking, if sex does not feel right to you on some particular occasion, don't engage in it. Follow your feelings in sexual matters even if you cannot always specify them completely.

Stephen M. Johnson

―――

The brain is viewed as an appendage of the genital glands.

Carl Jung

―――

Vain man is apt to think we (women) were merely intended for the World's propagation, and to keep its humane inhabitants sweet and clean; but by their leaves, had we the same Literature, he would find our brains as fruitful as our bodies.

Hannah Wooley

When a woman inclines to learning, there is usually something wrong with her sex apparatus.

Friedrich Nietzsche

―――

In general all curvaceousness strikes men as incompatible with the life of the mind.

Françoise Parturier

―――

Be to her virtues very kind;
Be to her faults a little blind;
Let all her ways be unconfin'd;
And clap your padlock—on her mind.

Matthew Prior

―――

Man is born to be intellectual, thus to think from the understanding; woman is born to be voluntary, thus to think from the will.

Emanuel Swedenborg

―――

I didn't get ahead by sleeping with people. Girls, take heart!

Barbara Walters

―――

From a wealth of living I have proved
I must be silent, if I would be loved.

Anna Wickham

―――

But if God had wanted us to think with our wombs, why did He give us a brain?

Clare Boothe Luce

Intercourse

Coition is a slight attack of apoplexy.

Democritus of Abdera

The sexual act has no resemblance to any other act: its demands are frenzied and participate in infinity. It is a tidal wave able to cover everything and bear away everything.

François Mauriac

Intercourse is an assertion of mastery, one that announces his own higher caste and proves it upon a victim who is expected to surrender, serve, and be satisfied.

Kate Millett

Let's take coitus out of the closet and off the altar and put it in the continuum of human behavior.

John Updike

Why do we fear to speak without shame of the act of generation, so natural, so necessary and so just; why do we exclude it from our serious and regular discourses?

Michel de Montaigne

148

In sexual intercourse it's quality not quantity that counts.

David Reuben

. . .even on the level of simply physical sensation and mood, making love surely resembles having an epileptic fit at least as much, if not more, than it does eating a meal or conversing with someone.

Rosalie Sorrels

Now in this usual function of the sexes which brings male and female together—I mean, in ordinary intercourse—we know that the soul and the body both take part; the soul through the desire, the body through its realization, the soul through the impulse, the body through the act.

Tertullian

Of the delights of this world man cares most for sexual intercourse. He will go any length for it—risk fortune, character, reputation, life itself. And what do you think he has done? In a thousand years you would never guess—He has left it out of his heaven! Prayer takes its place.

Mark Twain

K

Kindness
Kissing

Kindness

As in all other experiences, we always have the sexual experience we deserve, depending on our loving kindness towards ourselves and others.

Thaddeus Golas

In hotel bedrooms I learnt to call people toi, and I learnt a vast, all-embracing kindness for men—men sweating or coughing, handsome or ugly, sunburnt or pale, who all smoked after they made love. The time of shady hotels with their creaking lifts and dangling wallpaper is past, but I have never forgotten that kindness.

Françoise Mallet-Joris

The man that lays his hand on women,
Save in the way of kindness, is a wretch
Whom 'twere gross flattery to name a coward.

John Tobin

Many kiss the child for love of the nurse.

Thomas Wright

Kissing

Some women blush when they are kissed; some call for the police; some swear, some bite. But the worst are those who laugh.

Anonymous

Kissing an unwilling pair of lips is as mean a victory as robbing a bird's nest, and kissing too willing ones is about as unfragrant a recreation as making bouquets out of dandelions.

Josh Billings

Do not make me kiss, and you will not make me sin.

H. G. Bohn

And when my lips meet thine
Thy very soul is wedded unto mine.

H. H. Boyesen

A winning kiss she gave,
A long one, with a free and yielding lip.

William Browne

Their lips drew near, and clung into a kiss;
A long, long kiss of youth and love. . .
Each kiss a heart-quake,—for a kiss's strength,
I think, it must be reckon'd by its length.

George Gordon Byron

How delicious is the winning
Of a kiss at Love's beginning.

Thomas Campbell

My child, if you finally decide to let a man kiss you, put your
whole heart and soul into it. No man likes to kiss a rock.

Lady Chesterfield

Oh, fie, Miss, you must not kiss and tell.

Congreve

Kisses kept are wasted;
Love is to be tasted.

Edmund Vance Cooke

She that will kiss, they say, will do worse.

Robert Davenport

The kiss originated when the first male reptile licked the first female reptile, implying in a subtle, complimentary way that she was as succulent as the small reptile he had for dinner the night before.

F. Scott Fitzgerald

Kisses may not spread germs, but they certainly lower resistance.

Louise Erickson

Rose kissed me today.
  Will she kiss me tomorrow?
Let it be as it may,
Rose kissed me today.

Austin Dobson

(A kiss is) the anatomical juxtaposition of two orbicularis oris muscles in a state of contraction.

Henry Gibbons

A kiss is worth nothing until it's divided between two.

Gypsy proverb

When a rogue kisses you, count your teeth.

Hebrew proverb

Give me a kiss and to that kiss a score;
Then to that twenty add a hundred more;
A thousand to that hundred; so kiss on,
To make that thousand up a million;
Treble that million, and when that is done,
Let's kiss afresh as when we first begun.

Robert Herrick

You kissed me! My head drooped low on your breast
With a feeling of shelter and infinite rest,
While the holy emotions my tongue dared not speak
Flashed up as a flame from my heart to my cheek.

Josephine Slogum Hunt

Only he felt he could no more dissemble,
And kissed her, mouth to mouth, all in a tremble.

Leigh Hunt

Drink to me only with thine eyes,
  And I will pledge with mine;
Or leave a kiss but in the cup,
  And I'll not look for wine.

Ben Jonson

Be touchable and kissable.

Marabel Morgan

A kiss can be a comma, a question mark or an exclamation point. That's basic spelling that every woman ought to know.

Mistinguett

And our lips found ways of speaking
   What words cannot say,
Till a hundred nests gave music,
   And the East was gray.

Frederic Lawrence Knowles

Sweet Helen, make me immortal with a kiss! Her lips suck forth my soul: see, where it flies!

Christopher Marlowe

A little time for laughter,
   A little time to sing,
   A little time to kiss and cling,
And no more kissing after.

P. B. Marston

Give me another naughty, naughty kiss before we part.

Plautus

A soft Lip,
Would tempt you to eternity of kissing!

Ben Jonson

He who has taken kisses, if he take not the rest beside, deserves to lose even what was granted.

Ovid

—————

For love or lust, for good or ill,
Behold the kiss is potent still.

John Richard Moreland

—————

Take me by the earlaps and match my little lips to your little lips.

Plautus

—————

When women kiss it always reminds one of prize fighters shaking hands.

H. L. Mencken

—————

The lips of a strange woman drop as a honey-comb, and her mouth is smoother than oil.

Proverbs

—————

You can't kiss a girl unexpectedly—only sooner than she thought you would.

Jack Seaman

A kiss, when all is said, what is it?
            . . .a rosy dot
Placed on the "i" in loving; 'tis a secret
Told to the mouth instead of to the ear.

Edmond Rostand

She kissed his brow, his cheek, his chin,
And where she ends she doth anew begin.

Shakespeare

Take, O take those lips away,
   That so sweetly were forsworn;
And those eyes, the break of day,
   Lights that do mislead the morn;
But my kisses bring again, bring again;
Seals of love, but seal'd in vain, seal'd in vain.

Shakespeare

My lips till then had only known
   The kiss of mother and of sister,
But somehow, full upon her own
   Sweet rosy, darling mouth,—I kissed her.

E. C. Stedman

The woman that cries hush bids kiss: I learnt
So much of her that taught me kissing.

Swinburne

Though I know he loves me,
  Tonight my heart is sad;
His kiss was not so wonderful
  As all the dreams I had.

                              Sara Teasdale

━━━━━━━

Stephon's kiss was lost in jest,
  Robin's lost in play,
But the kiss in Colin's eyes
  Haunts me night and day.

                              Sara Teasdale

━━━━━━━

When I was very young, I kissed my first woman, and smoked
my first cigarette on the same day. Believe me, never since
have I wasted any more time on tobacco.

                              Arturo Toscanini

━━━━━━━

Many an evening by the waters did we watch
  the stately ships,
And our spirits rush'd together at the touching
  of the lips.

                              Alfred Lord Tennyson

━━━━━━━

Dear as remembered kisses after death,
And sweet as those by hopeless fancy feigned
On lips that are for others.

                              Alfred Lord Tennyson

Two people kissing always look like fish.

Andy Warhol

Few men know how to kiss well; fortunately, I've always had time to teach them.

Mae West

Wanton kisses are the keys
Free of her lips, free of her hips.

John Ray

L

Law
Legs
Lesbianism
Lesbians
Love
Lovers
Loyalty
Lust
Lying

Law

The United States is unique in the world for the number and variety of its laws against sexual activity.

Bernhardt J. Hurwood

There are two kinds of moral law, two kinds of conscience, in man and woman, and they are altogether different. The two sexes do not understand each other. But in practical life, the woman is judged by man's law, as if she were a man, not a woman.

Henrik Ibsen

It is horrible to listen to men in black togas (in court) having discussions about your morals, your cystitis, your feelings, your womb, the way you straddled your legs.

Gigliola Pierobon

All that is good and commendable now existing would continue to exist if all marriage laws were repealed tomorrow. . . . I have an inalienable constitutional and natural right to love whom I may, to love as long or as short a period as I can, to change that love every day if I please.

Victoria Calvin Woodhull

Legs

I am not in the least disturbed when people regard my legs intently. I know they are doing so in pursuance of their inherent artistic instinct.

Marlene Dietrich

The average man is more interested in a woman who is interested in him than he is in a woman with beautiful legs.

Marlene Dietrich

There are two reasons why I'm in show business, and I'm standing on both of them.

Betty Grable

Perhaps at 14 every boy should be in love with some ideal woman to put on a pedestal and worship. As he grows up, of course, he will put her on a pedestal the better to view her legs.

Barry Norman

Lesbianism

Lesbianism is far more than a sexual preference: it is a political stance.

Sidney Abbott

Love between women is seen as a paradigm of love between equals, and that is perhaps its greatest attraction.

Elizabeth Janeway

Feminism at heart is a massive complaint. Lesbianism is the solution.

Jill Johnston

There is nothing mysterious or magical about lesbian love-making. . . . The mystery and the magic come from the person with whom you are making love.

Del Martin

To understand the lesbian as a sexual being,
One must understand woman as a sexual being.

Del Martin

At a time when women, the forgotten sex, are voicing their rage and demanding their personhood, it is fitting that we (lesbians) emerge from the shadows.

Del Martin

I have no doubt that lesbianism makes a woman virile and open to any sexual stimulation, and that she is more often than not a more adequate and lively partner in bed than a "normal" woman.

Charlotte Wolff

Lesbians

Girls who put out are tramps. Girls who don't are ladies. This is however, a rather archaic use of the word. Should one of you boys happen upon a girl who doesn't put out, do not jump to the conclusion that you have found a lady. What you have probably found is a lesbian.

Fran Lebowitz

Were kisses all the joys in bed,
One woman would another wed.

Shakespeare

Refusal to make herself the object is not always what turns women to homosexuality; most lesbians, on the contrary, seek to cultivate the treasures of their femininity.

Simone de Beauvoir

What's the point of being a lesbian if a woman is going to look and act like an imitation man?

Rita Mae Brown

Once you know what women are like, men get kind of boring. I'm not trying to put them down, I mean I like them sometimes as people, but sexually they're dull.

Rita Mae Brown

. . .a woman who wants a woman usually wants a woman.

Sidney Abbott

168

In the forties, to get a girl you had to be a GI or a jock. In the fifties, to get a girl you had to be Jewish. In the sixties, to get a girl you had to be black. In the seventies, to get a girl you've got to be a girl.

Mort Sahl

Love

The prerequisite for making love is to like someone enormously.

Helen Gurley Brown

A quarter hour's physical intimacy between two persons of different sexes who feel for each other, I won't say love, but liking, creates a trust, a tender interest that the most devoted friendship does not inspire even when it has lasted ten years.

Senac de Meilhan

Just as you can't cook without heat you can't make love without feedback (which may be the reason we say "make love" rather than "make sex").

Alex Comfort

No growth of understanding, which has not love as its centre, can ever claim to fulfill adequately the spiritual, psychological and physical requirements on this subject.

J. Dominian

The only thing which is not purely mechanical about falling in love is its beginning. Although all those who fall in love do so in the same way, not all fall in love for the same reason. There is no single quality which is universally loved.

Ortega Y Gasset

Love is the answer. But while you're waiting for the answer, sex raises some pretty good questions.

Woody Allen

There is nothing enduring in life for a woman except what she builds in a man's heart.

Judith Anderson

Love had brought her here, to lie beside this young man; love was the key to every good; love lay like a mirage through the golden gates of sex.

Doris Lessing

Real personal love is the basis in the absence of which sexual relations are unchaste and immoral.

John MacMurray

When sex is divided from love there is a feeling that one has been stopped at the vestibule of the castle of pleasure; that the heart has been denied the city after crossing the bridge.

Fulton J. Sheen

Between two human beings who love one another, the sexual relationship is one of the possible expressions of love. . . . It is neither something high and holy, something to venerate and be proud of, nor is it something low and contemptible, to be ashamed of. It is a simple organic function to be used like all the others, for the expression of personality in the service of love.

John MacMurray

You mustn't force sex to do the work of love or love to do the work of sex.

Mary McCarthy

Love is the only circumstance in which the female is (ideologically) pardoned for sexual activity.

Kate Millett

Love between man and woman is a psychosomatic activity which consumes energy and wastes time. On the other hand, love of the Chairman takes no time at all, and is in itself a powerful tonic.

The Peking Workers' Daily

The beauty of love. . .vanishes if its mere physical expression be consciously sought as a means of sensual gratification, without the spiritual and aesthetic accompaniments that alone give it human value.

Harry Roberts

(Sex is) a clever imitation of love. It has all the action but none of the plot.

William Rotsler

Love is something far more than desire for sexual intercourse; it is the principal means of escape from the loneliness which afflicts most men and women throughout the greater part of their lives.

Bertrand Russell

All love, however ethereally it may bear itself, is rooted in the sexual impulse alone, nay, it absolutely is only a more definitely determined, specialized, and indeed in the strictest sense individualized sexual impulse.

Arthur Schopenhauer

The greatest illusion of lovers is to believe that the intensity of their sexual attraction is the guarantee of the perpetuity of their love. It is because of this failure to distinguish between the glandular and the spiritual. . .that marriages are so full of deception.

Fulton J. Sheen

Lovers

There is no fury like a woman searching for a new lover.

Cyril Connolly

A beautiful woman once told her sullen, much-married-looking lover: When you are seen, monsieur, in society with my husband, you are expected to look more cheerful than he does.

Nicolas Chamfort

A lover . . .tries to stand in well with the pet dog of the house.

Molière

It is only when we have lost ourselves in the totally relaxed, glorious freedom of true love-making that we can begin to glimpse its life-enhancing nature, or the wonderful sense of peace and fulfilment which follows.

Derek & Julia Parker

It is easier to keep half-a-dozen lovers guessing than to keep one lover after he has stopped guessing.

Helen Rowland

'Tis strange what a man may do, and a woman yet think him an angel.

William Makepeace Thackeray

So far as woman is concerned there are no "great" lovers. The "great" lovers of the world have all been elected to this post either on their own recognizance or on the word of other men.

Jessamyn West

Most (lovers) lead lives of unquiet desperation, continually seeking, in sex they wish was love and in the love they suspect is only sex, a center for their worlds to turn on.

David Dempsey

You can change one lover for another, but not a husband.

Pierre Corneille

Every day men sleep with women whom they do not love, and do not sleep with women whom they do love.

Diderot

If Jack's in love, he's no judge of Jill's beauty.

Benjamin Franklin

Loyalty

A woman is more responsive to a man's forgetfulness than to his attentions.

Janin

She hugged the offender, and forgave
  the offense:
Sex to the last.

John Dryden

Oh if thou lovest
And art a woman, hide thy love from him
Whom thou dost worship. Never let him know
How dear he is.

Letitia Elizabeth Landon

When first her gentle bosom knows
　Love's flame, it wanders never,
Deep in her heart the passion glows;
　She loves, and loves forever!

Isaac Pocock

Lust

Sinful lust is not nature, but a disease of nature.

Saint Augustine

Lust is an appetite by which temporal goods are preferred to eternal goods.

Saint Augustine

I define charity as a motion of the soul whose purpose is to enjoy God for His own sake and one's self and one's neighbor for the sake of God. Lust, on the other hand is a motion of the soul bent upon enjoying one's self, one's neighbor, and any creature without reference to God.

Saint Augustine

Whosoever looketh on a woman to lust after her hath committed adultery with her already in his heart.

The Bible

Love not the world, neither the things that are in the world. If any man love the world, the love of the Father is not in him.

For all that is in the world, the lust of the flesh, and the lust of the eyes, and the pride of life, is not of the Father, but is of the world.

And the world passeth away, and the lust thereof: but he that doeth the will of God abideth for ever

The Bible

I've looked on a lot of women with lust. I've committed adultery in my heart many times. This is something God recognizes I will do—and I have done it—and God forgives me for it. But that doesn't mean that I condemn someone who not only looks on a woman with lust but who leaves his wife and shacks up with someone out of wedlock.

Jimmy Carter

Too often the saint has agreed with the debauchee that the only difference between married love and lust is that love is allowed and the other is not.

Sydney Cave

From lust comes grief, from lust comes fear; he that is free from lust knows neither grief nor fear.

Dhammapada

As rain breaks through an ill-thatched roof, so lust breaks through an ill-trained mind.

Dhammapada

Lust should be stifled, for it cannot lead to truth.

Moses IBN Ezra

Like a fierce wind roaring high up in the bare branches of trees, a wave of passion came over me, aimless but surging. . . . I suppose it's lust but it's awful and holy like thunder and lightning and the wind.

Joanna Field

Poverty cannot disgrace the wise, nor can lust enslave them.

IBN Gabirol

Lust and reason are enemies.

IBN Gabirol

Lust is. . .both prevalent and reprehensible; but it may be doubted whether it does as much harm in the world day by day as the less socially disreputable misdemeanors of anger and envy.

Alfred Graham

A wanton and lascivious eye betrays the heart's adultery.

Robert Herrick

Lust is pursued by foolish men because of the immediacy of its delight. . .they ignore the suffering and wretchedness that follow in its train.

IBN Gabirol

He gave her a look you could have poured on a waffle.

Ring Lardner

He says his lust is in his heart. I hope it's a little lower.

Shirley MacLaine

Sexual lust ties us up like a rope.

Mahabharata

When lust
By unchaste looks, loose gestures, and foul talk,
But most by leud and lavish act of sin,
Lets in defilement to the inward parts,
The soul grows clotted by contagion,
Imbodies, and imbrutes, till she quite loose
The divine property of her first being.

John Milton

Lust has become natural to us and has made our second nature. Thus there are two natures in us—the one good, the other bad. Where is God? Where you are not, and the kingdom of God is within you.

Pascal

What is essentially wrong with lust is not that the body is used carnally but that the situation is such, the human relations are such, that this particular use of the body is the implementation of a wrong spirit.

James A. Pike

The love of a harlot, that is to say, the lust of sexual intercourse, which arises from mere external form, and absolutely all love which recognizes any other cause than the freedom of the mind, easily passes into hatred, unless, which is worse, it becomes a species of delirium, and thereby discord is cherished rather than concord.

Spinoza

Lust is like rot in the bones.

Talmud

Lust is what makes you keep wanting to do it, even when you have no desire to be with each other. Love is what makes you keep wanting to be with each other, even when you have no desire to do it.

Judith Viorst

Lust is the oldest lion of them all.

Marjorie Allen Seiffert

Love is all truth, Lust full of forged lies.

Shakespeare

Fie on sinful fantasy!
Fie on lust and luxury!
Lust is but a bloody fire,
Kindled with unchaste desire,
Fed in heart, whose flames aspire
As thoughts do blow them, higher and higher.

Shakespeare

I'd call it love if love didn't take so many years, but lust too is
a jewel.

Adrienne Rich

Lying

Very few people openly tell the truth about sex. I would say
that more people lie about sex than about any other subject
being dealt with today.

Albert Z. Freedman

Were women never so fair, men would be false.
Were women never so false, men would be fond.

John Lyly

A man who won't lie to a woman has very little consideration
for her feelings.

Olin Miller

All this humorless document (the Kinsey report) really proves is: (a) that all men lie when they are asked about their adventures in amour, and (b) that pedagogues are singularly naive and credulous creatures.

H. L. Mencken

For never was it given to mortal man
To lie so boldly as we women can.

Alexander Pope

Telling lies is a fault in a boy, an art in a lover, an accomplishment in a bachelor, and second nature in a married woman.

Helen Rowland

A man no more believes a woman when she says she has an aversion for him than when she says she'll cry out.

William Wycherley

You know how Americans are—when it comes to sex, the man can't keep from lying and the women can't keep from telling the truth.

Robin Zander

M

Manliness

Marriage

Masturbation

Memory

Mistresses

Money

Monogamy

Morality

Motivation

Manliness

The old man, especially if he is in society, in the privacy of his thoughts, though he may protest the opposite, never stops believing that, through some singular exception of the universal rule, he can in some unknown and inexplicable way still make an impression on women.

Giacomo Leopardi

There's a fine line between seducer and stud, and men who require women to be instruments become instruments themselves.

Merle Shain

The maternal instinct leads a woman to prefer a tenth share in a first rate man to the exclusive possession of a third rate one.

George Bernard Shaw

Marriage

To avoid fornication, let every man have his own wife, and let every woman have her own husband.

The Bible

If a man entice a maid that is not betrothed, and lie with her, he shall surely endow her to be his wife.

The Bible

When you get married you forget about kissing other women.

Pat Boone

"Adam knew Eve his wife and she conceived." It is a pity that this is still the only knowledge of their wives at which some men seem to arrive.

Francis Herbert Bradley

Married love is a creative enterprise. It is not achieved by accident or instinct. Perfunctory coitus is a confession of lack of intelligence and character. There is a profound beauty and even holiness in the act of fecundation.

Alexis Carrel

Take a wife for her virtue and a concubine for her beauty.

Chinese proverb

They've asked me everything but how often I sleep with my husband. And if they'd asked me that, I would have told them, "As often as possible."

Betty Ford

In a society which really supported marriage, the wife would be encouraged to go to the office and make love to her husband on the company's time and with its blessing.

Brendan Francis

More belongs to Marriage than four bare Legs in a Bed.

Thomas Fuller

It is a mistake for a taciturn, serious-minded woman to marry a jovial man, but not for a serious-minded man to marry a lighthearted woman.

Johann W. von Goethe

The real theatre of the sex was in the domestic hearth.

Germaine Greer

If men knew how women pass the time when they are alone, they'd never marry.

O. Henry

Although connubial intercourse with one's wife is always permitted, this relation should be invested by the scholar with sanctity. He should not always be with his spouse, like a rooster.

Maimonides

A miserable marriage can wobble along for years until something comes along and pushes one of the people over the brink. It's usually another man or woman.

Pat Loud

———

Love-making is radical, while marriage is conservative.

Eric Hoffer

———

Whoever cannot bridle his carnal affections, let him keep them within the bounds of lawful wedlock.

Lactantius

———

After twenty years of marriage I don't know how to handle men yet.

Pat Loud

———

A man marries to have a home, but also because he doesn't want to be bothered with sex and all that sort of thing.

Somerset Maugham

———

Love, for too many people in our time, consists of sleeping with a seductive woman, one who is properly endowed with the right distribution of curves and conveniences, and one upon whom a permanent lien has been acquired through the institution of marriage.

Ashley Montagu

There is never any real sex in romance; what is more, there is very little, and that of a very crude kind, in ninety-nine hundredths of our married life.

George Bernard Shaw

======

Chains do not hold a marriage together. It is threads, hundreds of tiny threads which sew people together through the years. That is what makes a marriage last—more than passion or even sex!

Simone Signoret

======

He who can't do any better goes to bed with his own wife.

Spanish proverb

======

Why does a woman work ten years to change a man's habits and then complain that he's not the man she married?

Barbra Streisand

======

I've only slept with the men I've been married to. How many women can make that claim?

Elizabeth Taylor

======

She said he proposed something on their wedding night her own brother wouldn't have suggested.

James Thurber

Two women. One when alone is exactly the same as she is in company, the other in company exactly what she is when she is alone. The latter holds herself badly in public, the former puts on evening dress when she dines by herself. One should marry neither.

Paul Valéry

———

The ideal marriage is a marriage in which everything of one participates in everything of another, and basic to it all is receiving and giving through full sexual relationships.

John H. Vruwunk

———

Marriage was instituted by God himself for the purpose of preventing promiscuous intercourse of the sexes, for promoting domestic felicity, and for securing the maintenance and security of children.

Noah Webster

———

Niagara Falls is only the second biggest disappointment of the standard honeymoon.

Oscar Wilde

Masturbation

A niggling feeling of discomfort and unease follows masturbation, even in those who do not feel guilty about it.

Charlotte Wolff

I do not think that masturbation is a bad thing; for the first time women are shown involved with their bodies, which is what the women's movement is all about.

Christie Hefner

The good thing about masturbation is that you don't have to dress up for it.

Truman Capote

A woman occasionally is quite a serviceable substitute for masturbation. It takes an abundance of imagination, to be sure.

Karl Kraus

The victim of masturbation passes from one degree of imbecility to another, till all of the powers of the system, mental, physical and moral, are blotted out forever.

John Todd

Memory

There is sanctuary in reading, sanctuary in formal society, in the company of old friends, and in the giving of officious help to strangers, but there is no sanctuary in one bed from the memory of another.

Cyril Connolly

First you forget names, then you forget faces, then you forget to pull your zipper up, then you forget to pull your zipper down.

James Thurber

═══

And the best and the worst of this is
    That neither is most to blame,
If you've forgotten my kisses
    And I've forgotten your name.

Swinburne

═══

Men are odd creatures. Women have to wait. It's always been that way.

Warren Gilbert

Mistresses

In Paris, when God provides a beautiful woman, the devil at once retorts with a fool to keep her.

Barbey D'Aurevilly

═══

Next to the pleasure of making a new mistress is that of being rid of an old one.

William Wycherley

These were clever and beautiful women, often of good background, who through some breach of the moral code or the scandal of divorce had been socially ostracized but had managed to turn the ostracism into profitable account. Cultivated, endowed with civilized graces, they were frankly—kept women, but kept by one man only, or, at any rate, by one man at a time.

Cornelia Otis Skinner

I am his mistress. His work is his wife.

Marion Javits

It's not impossible to become bored in the presence of a mistress.

Stendhal

Money

If women didn't exist, all the money in the world would have no meaning.

Aristotle Onassis

The sexuo-economic relationship. . .sexualizes our industrial relationship and commercializes our sex-relation.

Charlotte Perkins Gilman

When they said that tickets for 'Hair' were $10 apiece I went into my bathroom, took off my clothes and looked in the mirror for ten minutes and said 'It isn't worth it'.

Groucho Marx

———

First secure an independent income, then practice virtue.

Greek proverb

———

One reason I hate the marriage system is that it's a business or it becomes one if it fails.

Goldie Hawn

———

About money and sex it is impossible to be truthful ever; one's ego is too involved.

Malcolm Muggeridge

———

In their hearts all women believe that it is the business of men to earn money and their own to spend it—if possible, while their husbands live, but if not, then afterward.

Arthur Schopenhauer

———

The prostitutes continue to take all the arrests, the police to suffer frustration, the lawyers to mine gold, the operators to laugh, the landowners to insist they have no responsibility, the mayor to issue press releases. The nature of the beast is, in a word, greed.

Gail Sheehy

Monogamy

If she refuses to have intercourse with one whom she dearly loves, not out of coyness, but through allegiance to a moral value, which is a real value to her, the potential of their love will mount behind the barrier she interposes.

M. Esther Harding

I don't like hippies. I don't like communes. I despise heroin. I've never participated in an orgy. It may ruin my reputation, but I'm particularly monogamous.

Timothy Leary

I've never bought that open marriage thing. I've never seen it work. But that doesn't mean I believe in monogamy. Sleeping with someone else doesn't necessarily constitute an infidelity. . .What does is having sex with someone and telling your spouse. . .anything you feel guilty about.

Carly Simon

Morality

I think anything is all right provided it is done in private and doesn't frighten the horses.

Brendan Behan

Modern man refuses to recognize that God has set certain standards, certain absolutes for sex, as he has for behavior generally. To be ignorant of these absolutes, or to deny them or rationalize them, in no way invalidates them.

L. Nelson Bell

Morality is a private and costly luxury.

Henry Adams

The popular morality is now a wasteland. It is littered with the debris of broken convictions. A new concept is emerging, of sexual relationships as a source of pleasure, but also as a mutual encountering of personalities in which each explores the other and at the same time discovers new depths in himself or herself.

George Morrison Carstairs

A woman can look both moral and exciting—if she also looks as if it was quite a struggle.

Edna Ferber

What is moral is what you feel good after and what is immoral is what you feel bad after.

Ernest Hemingway

Moralizing and morals are two entirely different things and are always found in entirely different people.

Don Herold

Sex is not a moral question. For answers you don't turn to a body of absolutes. The criterion should not be, "Is it morally right or wrong?" but "Is it socially feasible, is it personally healthy and rewarding, will it enrich life?"

Grancolle Fisher

When human beings are regarded as moral beings, sex, instead of being enthroned upon the summit, administrating upon rights and responsibilities, sinks into insignificance and nothingness. . .

Angelina Grimke

We grant the Freudian thesis that the repression of primitive instincts leads to neurosis; but the repression of moral aspirations often produces an identical effect.

Ignace Lepp

Perhaps when we know more we shall be able to say that the best sexual ethic will be quite different in one climate from what it would be in another, different again with one kind of diet than from what it would be with another.

Bertrand Russell

We are told by moralists with the plainest faces that immorality will spoil our looks.

Logan Pearsall Smith

———

Certainly nothing is unnatural that is not physically impossible.

Richard Brinsley Sheridan

———

All the things I really like to do are either immoral, illegal or fattening.

Alexander Woollcott

Motivation

(Sex is) a great and mysterious motive force in human life.

William Brennan, Jr.

———

In a society where people get more or less what they want sexually, it is much more difficult to motivate them in an industrialized context, to make them buy refrigerators and cars.

William S. Burroughs

How awkward it must be to love somebody and you don't know *why*.

Goldie Hawn

Many "highly sexed" individuals turn to sex, not because of desire, but because they have a need to prove how attainable or lovable they are.

Maj-Britt Rosenbaum

The sex instinct is one of the three or four prime movers of all that we do and are and dream, both individually and collectively.

Philip Wylie

N

Need
Nudity

Need

Long-term love expressed in active sex means you have to know something about the biology of people. Don't go in for mutual do-it-yourself psychoanalysis, or you'll bring down the roof on each other. We all have pregenital needs, however we were weaned, potted or reared, just as we all have fingerprints and a navel.

Alex Comfort

The starting point of all lovemaking is close bodily contact. Love has been defined as the harmony of two souls and the contact of two epiderms. It is also, from our infancy, the starting point of human relationships and needs.

Alex Comfort

If our elaborate and dominating bodies are given us to be denied at every turn, if our nature is always wrong and wicked, how ineffectual we are—like fishes not meant to swim.

Cyril Connolly

Sex is the last refuge of the miserable.

Quentin Crisp

Were there no women, men might live like gods.

Thomas Dekker

By the end of the first week of marriage even the most skeptical husband usually recognizes that his wife has sexual needs just as real as his own.

David R. Reuben

A woman without a man is like a garden without a fence.

German proverb

Books are helpful in bed. But they are not responsive (commenting on widowhood).

Mary Hemingway

As unto the bow the cord is,
So unto the man is woman;
Though she bends him she obeys him,
Though she draws him, yet she follows,
Useless each without the other.

Henry W. Longfellow

O woman! lovely woman! Nature made thee
To temper man: we had been brutes without you.

Thomas Otway

The judgment of sex in its modern idolatry becomes a testimony to man's need of the life and love which God alone can bestow, a witness to the reality it prefigures and reflects.

E. I. Watkin

As for the women, though we scorn and flout 'em,
We may live with, but cannot live without 'em.

Frederic Reynolds

He who believes in nothing still needs a girl to believe in him.

Rosenstock-Huessy

Failing to be there when a man wants her is a woman's greatest sin, except to be there when he doesn't want her.

Helen Rowland

O Woman! in our hours of ease
Uncertain, coy, and hard to please,
And variable as the shade
By the light quivering aspen made;
When pain and anguish wring the brow,
A ministering angel thou!

Walter Scott

Is Sex Necessary?

James Thurber

Men are obsessed by women who do not need them.

Gore Vidal

The two sexes mutually corrupt and improve each other.

Mary Wollstonecraft

A person who despises or undervalues or neglects the opposite sex will soon need humanizing.

Charles Simmons

Nudity

I wasn't really naked. I simply didn't have any clothes on.

Josephine Baker

There are those who so dislike the nude that they find something indecent in the naked truth.

Francis Herbert Bradley

For a woman to be loved, she usually ought to be naked.

Pierre Cardin

No woman so naked as one you can see to be naked underneath her clothes.

Michael Frayn

I think naked people are very nice. Posing in the nude is perhaps the best way of reaching people.

Stella Stevens

Let's all go out into the sunshine, take off our clothes, dance and sing and make love and get enlightened.

Alicia Bay Laurel

If it was the fashion to go naked, the face would be hardly observed.

Mary Wortley Montagu

'Tis an affect worth consideration, that they, who are masters in the trade, prescribe as a remedy for amorous passions the full and free view of the body a man desires; so that, to cool his ardour, there needs no more but at full liberty to see and contemplate what he loves.

Michel de Montaigne

Man is the sole animal whose nudities offend his own companions, and the only one who, in his natural actions, withdraws and hides himself from his own kind.

Michel de Montaigne

All women's dresses are merely variations on the eternal struggle between the admitted desire to dress and the unadmitted desire to undress.

Lin Yutang

O

Obscenity

Obsession

Oral Sex

Orgasm

Obscenity

Vulgarity begins when imagination succumbs to the explicit.

Doris Day

I'm never dirty. I'm interesting without being vulgar. I just. . . suggest.

Mae West

There are as many different definitions of the word obscenity as there are men.

Kathy Keeton

Obsession

The pace and range of modern life are reducing even domestic love to the status of a quick-lunch counter.

Rosita Forbes

Sexual obsessions are the basis of artistic creation.

Salvador Dali

We are all going to become Swedish, and we do not understand these Americans who, like adolescents, always speak of sex, and who, like adolescents, all of a sudden have discovered that sex is good not only for procreating children.

Oriana Fallaci

...with her overcharged sensibility, her prominent modesty, her "eternal feminity"—the female genus homo is undeniably oversexed.

Charlotte Perkins Gilman

America has a greater obsession with sex than Rome ever had.

Billy Graham

There are people who want to keep our sex instinct inflamed in order to make money out of us. Because, of course, a man with an obsession is a man who has very little sales-resistance.

C.S. Lewis

That our popular art forms become so obsessed with sex has turned the U.S.A. into a nation of hobbledehoys; as if grown people don't have more vital concerns, such as taxes, inflation, dirty politics, earning a living, getting an education, or keeping out of jail.

Anita Loos

The more holy he gets, the more his books stink with sex. He cannot get off the subject of flagellating women.

George Orwell,
writing about Aldous L. Huxley

———

. . .we've never been in a democracy; we've always been in a phallocracy!

Françoise Parturier

———

Our tawdry doting on sex—quick to the soonest bed!—is an erotic rotting of gratitude that makes a travesty of love, a travesty of the wonder and joy of love that waits only upon our gratitude to be born in the great antiphonal song of man and woman, which no other creature on earth knows and sings.

Robert Reynolds

———

Women do not properly understand that when an idea fills and elevates a man's mind it shuts out love and crowds out people.

Jean Paul Richter

———

Sex is the tabasco sauce which an adolescent national palate sprinkles on every course in the menu.

Mary Day Winn

Oral Sex

From Ovid downwards, western authors have ever treated the subject (oral congress) jocularly or with a tendency to hymn the joys of immorality, and the gospel of debauchery.

Henry Spencer Ashbee (Pisanus Fraxi)

Countless, countless, countless people in this country would never have known of oral sex if it had not been forced into their consciousness by the media, and many, many people will find this distasteful.

Mortimer Caplan

Every couple committed to a loving relationship, every man and woman searching for a meaningful relationship and every person who wishes temporary—but caring—alliances can utilize oral love and its major form of expression for lovers, oral sex, to construct their own pleasure-bond.

Emily Coleman

I see a lot of porn flicks and I don't think I've seen any in the past few years that weren't 70 or 80 percent oral sex.

Andrew Harris

The oral aspects of love have been an essential and dynamic part of intimate relations since the dawn of civilization.

Bernhardt J. Hurwood

All the statistics show that 95 percent of all people have engaged in some form of oral intercourse at one time or another.

David Parot

Cunnilingus and fellatio. . .have not thus far been shown to depend upon psychopathological conditions. These horrible sexual acts seem to be committed only by sensual men who have become satiated or impotent from excessive indulgence in a normal way.

Richard von Krafft-Ebing

Orgasm

Orgasm is the most obvious lie yet devised to thwart man. It can so thoroughly convince him of something which is unreal when he believes that the power of his excitement lies somewhere other than in his own physical apparatus.

William Talsman

A woman's reaching orgasm means giving up her hold on the world around her. In a woman who subconsciously feels that people and things are undependable or transitory, this fading process can be so alarming that it can prevent sexual excitement from building up.

Seymour Fisher

———

Sexual technology could best be served by orgasms which came on the beat of society's best machines.

Norman Mailer

———

In the vast majority of marriages where sex is a problem, it's usually assumed that it's the wife who needs help.

William H. Masters

———

The orgasm has replaced the Cross as the focus of longing and the image of fulfillment.

Malcolm Muggeridge

———

Orgasms really have very little to do with making love, and men who require their women to respond with a *petit mal* seizure that can be picked up on the Richter scale are not making love but asking for reassurance.

Merle Shain

When modern woman discovered the orgasm it was (combined with modern birth control) perhaps the biggest single nail in the coffin of male dominance.

Eva Figes

All orgasms are created equal.

David M. Reuben

The nature of female sexuality as here presented makes it clear that. . .woman's inordinate orgasmic capacity did not evolve for monogamous, sedentary cultures.

Mary Jane Sherfey

There is no such thing as a vaginal orgasm distinct from a clitoral orgasm. The nature of the orgasm is the same regardless of the erotogenic zone stimulated to produce it.

Mary Jane Sherfey

P

Passion

Penis

Performance

Perversion

Pill, The

Pleasure

Pornography

Power, Sexual

Preferences, Sexual

Premarital Sex

Pride

Procreation

Promiscuity

Prostitution

Prudery

Puritanism

Purity

Passion

The duration of passion is proportionate with the original resistance of the woman.

Honoré de Balzac

It subverts kingdoms, overthrows cities, towns, families; mars, corrupts and makes a massacre of men; thunder and lightning, wars, fires, plagues, have not done that mischief as this burning lust, this brutish passion.

Robert Burton

We are n'er like angels till our passion dies.

Thomas Dekker

Even a shower of gold cannot secure satisfaction of our passions. He who realizes that passions give brief enjoyment and can produce such distress, is wise.

Dhammapada

The passion of a heedless man grows like a creeper, and he runs from life to life, like a monkey seeking fruit in the forest.

Dhammapada

A man in a passion rides a wild horse.

Benjamin Franklin

When passion burns within you, remember that it was given to you for good purposes.

Hasidic saying

Passion has as much conscience as a worm entering a luscious apple.

Paul Eldridge

Passion, joined with power, produceth thunder and ruin.

Thomas Fuller

Man is in bondage to his passions—and his Creator.

Hasidic saying

Passion leads to prejudice, not reason.

Hasidic saying

The pursuit of passion becomes boring.

Hasidic saying

Passion is a master.

Hasidic saying

Passions unguided are for the most part mere madness.

Thomas Hobbes

We may affirm absolutely that nothing great in the world has been accomplished without passion.

Georg Wilhelm Friedrich Hegel

A correspondence course of passion was, for her, the perfect and ideal relationship with a man.

Aldous Huxley

(Passion is) a burning forehead and a parching tongue.

John Keats

Passion often turns the cleverest men into idiots and makes the greatest blockheads clever.

La Rochefoucauld

The most beautiful make-up of a woman is a passion. But cosmetics are easier to buy.

Yves Saint Laurent

A man and a woman may want one another passionately without either loving the other.

John MacMurray

(Passion is) a sort of fever in the mind, which leaves us weaker than it found us.

William Penn

It is with our passions, as it is with fire and water; they are good servants but bad masters.

Roger L'Estrange

Mortal lovers must not try to remain at the first step; for lasting passion is the dream of a harlot and from it we wake in despair.

C. S. Lewis

In spite of his age and strong passions he (D.H. Lawrence) had never let himself go. Sex was suppressed in him with ferocity. He had suppressed it so much, put it away so entirely, that now, married, it overwhelmed him.

Frieda Lawrence

Our passions are like travelers: at first they make a brief stay; then they are like guests, who visit often; and then they turn into tyrants, who hold us in their power.

Talmud

At first, man's passions are like a cobweb's thread; at last, they become like thickest cord.

Talmud

There is always something ridiculous about the passions of people whom one has ceased to love.

Oscar Wilde

Penis

The penis is the only muscle man has that he cannot flex. It is also the only extremity he cannot control. . . But even worse, as it affects the dignity of its owner, is its seeming obedience to that inferior thing, woman. It rises at the sight, or even at the thought of a woman.

Elizabeth Gould Davis

Don't forget, the penis is mightier than the sword.

Screamin' Jay Hawkins

The penis is obviously going the way of the veriform appendix.

Jill Johnston

Despite the fact that she had had no sexual experience, she had a very clear idea of the male member, and she could not help forming a picture of Put's as pale and lifeless, in the coffin of his trousers, a veritable nature morte.

Mary McCarthy

I wonder why men can get serious at all. They have this delicate long thing hanging outside their bodies, which goes up and down by its own will. . . . If I were a man I would always be laughing at myself.

Yoko Ono

That the most intelligent, discerning and learned men, men of talent and feeling, should finally put all their pride in their crotch, as awed as they are uneasy at the few inches sticking out in front of them, proves how normal it is for the world to be crazy. . .

Françoise Parturier

There was never any reason to believe in any innate superiority of the male, except his superior muscle.

Bertrand Russell

Man has a small organ; the more he feeds it the more it needs—and vice versa.

Talmud

If you have a psychotic fixation and you go to the doctor and you want these two fingers amputated, he will not cut them off. But he will remove your genitals. I have more trouble getting a prescription for Valium than I do having my uterus lowered and made into a penis.

Lily Tomlin

Whether, as some psychologists believe, some women suffer from penis envy, I am not sure. I am quite certain, however, that all males without exception suffer from penis rivalry, and that this trait has become a threat to the future existence of the human race.

W. H. Auden

No woman, except for so-called "deviants" seriously wishes to be male and have a penis. But most women would like to have the privileges and opportunities that go with it.

Eliana Gianini Belotti

In most marriages, at some time, a husband or wife will refuse lovemaking because of distraction, excitement or, most likely, personal hurt. This is a powerful weapon because it touches the innermost sensitivities of the partner. But it is a weapon that should never be used. To do so is a sin against the spirit.

Marion Hilliard

Performance

A little theory makes sex more interesting, more comprehensible, and less scary—too much is a put-down, especially as you're likely to get it out of perspective and become a spectator of your own performance.

Alex Comfort

A man is as good as he has to be, and a woman as bad as she dares.

Elbert Hubbard

There are no unseduceable women—only inept men.

Melina Mercouri

They say all lovers swear more performances than they are able and yet reserve an ability that they never perform, vowing more than the perfection of ten and discharging less than the tenth part of one.

Shakespeare

A woman is a woman until the day she dies, but a man's a man only as long as he can.

Moms Mabley

Once they call you a Latin Lover, you're in real trouble. Women expect an Oscar performance in bed.

Marcello Mastroianni

Is it not strange that desire should so many years outlive performance?

Shakespeare

Perversion

The only unnatural sex act is that which you cannot perform.
Alfred Kinsey

Society is like sex in that no one knows what perversions it can develop once aesthetic considerations are allowed to dictate its choices.

Marcel Proust

Sex perversion or any inference of it is forbidden. White slavery shall not be treated. Miscegenation is forbidden. Sex hygiene and veneral diseases are not subjects for motion pictures. Scenes of actual childbirth, in fact or in silhouette, are never to be represented. Children's sex organs are never to be exposed.

Motion Picture Code, 1930

It is our intention to keep the hellgate of the realm of sexual perversion firmly closed. . .all that is morbid, all that is perverse we banished, for this is holy ground.

Theodor Hendrik Van DeVelde

Pill, The

With almost all doctors, population experts, and drug manufacturers male, is it really a surprise that oral contraceptives were designed for women to take and men to promote?

Ellen Frankfort

If I became dictator of the world I'd give all the poor a cottage and birth control pills—and I'd make damn sure they didn't get one if they didn't take the other!

Lyndon B. Johnson

No woman should be kept on the Pill for twenty years until, in fact, a sufficient number have been kept on the Pill for twenty years.

Sir Alan Sterling Parks

Pleasure

Sensual pleasures have the fleeting brilliance of a comet; a happy marriage has the tranquility of a lovely sunset.

Ann Landers

Sexual pleasure, wisely used and not abused, may prove the stimulus and liberator of our finest and most exalted activities.

Havelock Ellis

(Sex is) a catalog of many pleasures.

Warren Goldberg

Graze on my lips, and when those mounts are dry
Stray lower, where the pleasant fountains lie.

Gervase Markham

Our extremest pleasure has some air of groaning and complaining in it; would you not say that it is dying of pain?

Michel de Montaigne

Pleasure is more trouble than trouble.

Don Herold

It is a fact terrible to contemplate, yet it is nevertheless true, and ought to be pressed upon the world for its recognition; that full one-half of all women seldom or never experience any pleasure whatever in the sexual act. Now this is an impeachment of nature, a disgrace to our civilization.

Victoria Claflin Woodhull

What lively lad most pleasured me
Of all that with me lay?
I answer that I gave my soul
And loved in misery,
But had great pleasure with a lad
That I loved bodily.

William Butler Yeats

No one can constantly sleep with his wife and take heartfelt pleasure in it.

Nicharchus

Show business is like sex. When it's wonderful, it's wonderful. But when it isn't very good, it's still all right.

Max Wall

Pleasure is frail like a dewdrop; while it laughs it dies.

Rabindranath Tagore

There are some elements in life—above all, sexual pleasure—about which it isn't necessary to have a position.

Susan Sontag

I do not believe in doing for pleasure things I do not like to do.

Don Herold

Pornography

Sex and obscenity are not synonymous. Obscene material is material which deals with sex in a manner appealing to prurient interest.

William Brennan, Jr.

The value difference between pornographic playing cards when you're a kid, and pornographic playing cards when you're older: it's that when you're a kid you use cards as a substitute for a real experience, and when you are older you use real experience as a substitute for the fantasy.

Edward Albee

Pornography is not in the hands of the child who discovers his sexuality by masturbating, but in the hands of the adult who slaps him.

Bernardo Bertolucci

An individual's becoming aroused by perusing or reading pornographic sex material is certainly one of the most common of all sex acts; and, in our puritanical society, which places a premium on open displays of sexuality precisely by banning them, any person who shows a reasonable degree of interest in pornographic representations is certainly normal and non-deviated.

Albert Ellis

If all the men who enjoy pornography were to "come out of the closet," there'd be no males, under ten, left in the house.

Brendan Francis

A sodomite got very excited looking at a zoology text. Does this make it pornography?

Stanislaw J. Lec

A taste for dirty stories may be said to be inherent in the human animal.

George Moore

Experiences aren't pornographic; only images and representations—structures of the imagination—are.

Rosalie Sorrels

I never knew a girl who was ruined by a bad book.

Jimmy Walker

Nine-tenths of the appeal of pornography is due to the indecent feelings concerning sex which moralists inculate in the young; the other tenth is physiological, and will occur in one way or another whatever the state of the law may be.

Bertrand Russell

Someone once remarked that in adolescence pornography is a substitute for sex, whereas in adulthood sex is a substitute for pornography.

Edmund White

Power, Sexual

The woman is the glory of the man.

The Bible

Here's to woman! Would that we could fall into her arms without falling into her hands.

Ambrose Bierce

Man's fate and woman's are contending powers;
Each tries to dupe the other in the game.

E. G. Bulwer-Lytton

Women? I guess they ought to exercise Pussy Power.

Eldridge Cleaver

To use the word "sex" intelligently, means to connote by it more than a specific sensory excitement. It involves the whole affectional life of man, and a major part of his motive power in every realm of creativity.

Harry Emerson Fosdick

Nature has given women so much power that the law has very wisely given them little.

Samuel Johnson

To the mind of the modern girl, legs, like busts, are power points which she has been taught to tailor, but as parts of the success kit rather than erotically or sensuously.

Marshall McLuhan

The sex organ has a poetic power, like a comet.

Joan Miro

Sex is just about the most powerful and explosive force that is built into us. Every instinct and every bit of counseling experience I have had tells me that it is too dangerous a commodity to be handed over to people with no strings attached.

Norman Vincent Peale

For the very reason that sexual power is so noble and necessary a good, it needs the preserving and defending order of
reason.

Josef Pieper

======

The men who really wield, retain, and covet power are the
kind who answer bedside phones while making love.

Nicholas Pileggi

======

The more potent a man becomes in the bedroom,
the more potent he is in business.

David Reuben

======

Men care about power because for them power is linked to
sexual performance. Women achieve positions of power out
of a need to do something, not because we need reassurance.

Karin Soeder

======

Desire looks clear from the eyes of a lovely bride: power as
strong as the founded world.

Sophocles

======

Traditionally, sex has been a very private, secretive activity.
Herein perhaps lies its powerful force for uniting people in a
strong bond. As we make sex less secretive, we may rob it of
its power to hold men and women together.

Thomas Szasz

The man experiences the unfolding of his creative powers not through asceticism but through sexual happiness.

Mathilda von Kemnitz

It is youth that has discovered love as a weapon.

Peter Ustinov

The best way to hold a man is in your arms.

Mae West

Preferences, Sexual

I had rather live with the woman I love in a world full of trouble, than to live in heaven with nobody but men.

R. G. Ingersoll

Sensible men prefer evening to morning, night to day, and mature women to young girls.

Paul Leautaud

I don't mind living in a man's world as long as I can be a woman in it.

Marilyn Monroe

Premarital Sex

I believe that the real issue about premarital sex is the risk of producing illegitimate children who from the start are denied the protection every human society has found it necessary to give.

Margaret Mead

It is fairly common in both young men and women with high standards of conduct and integrity to have one or two love affairs, involving intercourse, before they find the person they will ultimately marry. . . . Where there is genuine tenderness, an openness to responsibility and the seed of commitment, God is surely not shut out.

A group of the Religious Society of Friends, England.

Pride

A man would create another man if one did not already exist, but a woman might live an eternity without even thinking of reproducing her own sex.

Johann W. von Goethe

To find oneself jilted is a blow to one's pride. One must do one's best to forget it and if one doesn't succeed, at least one must pretend to.

Molière

Courtesans used to know more about the soul of men than any philosopher. The art is lost in the fog of snobbism and false respectability.

Elsa Schiaparelli

Procreation

The union of male and female for the purpose of procreation is the natural good of marriage. But he makes a bad use of this good who uses it bestially, so that his intention is on the gratification of lust, instead of the desire of offspring.

Saint Augustine

But I am aware of some that murmur: if all men should abstain from intercourse, how will the human race exist? Would that all would abstain; much more speedily would the City of God be filled, and the end of the world hastened.

Saint Augustine

What cures Morris makes Martha sick indeed nine months after.

Anonymous

It is wrong to leave a wife who is sterile in order to take another by whom children may be had. Anyone doing this is guilty of adultery.

Saint Augustine

(Sex is) an appetite placed in humans to insure breeding. It has in turn bred, as a side-product, interesting and often ludicrous customs. Its suppression has led to ugly perversions and cruelty.

Jonathan Benter

The sexual act takes on qualitative significance and value which transcends the other meanings the sexual act can have, when lovers use the act purposely to become parents. For now the two lovers express their faith in love itself, in the possibilities open to their children within the social order and in this world.

Peter A. Bertocci

To the woman He said, "I will greatly multiply your pain in child bearing; in pain you shall bring forth children yet your desire shall be for your husband, and he shall rule over you."

The Bible

The residue of virility in the woman's (sexual) organism is utilized by nature in order to eroticize her: otherwise the functioning of the maternal apparatus would wholly submerge her in the painful tasks of reproduction and motherhood.

Marie Bonaparte

Mirrors and copulation are abominable because they increase the numbers of men.

Jorge Luis Borges

I could be content that we might procreate like trees, without conjunction, or that there were any way to perpetrate the world without this trivial and vulgar way of coition; it is the foolishest act a wise man commits in all his life; nor is there any thing that will more deject his cool'd imagination, when he shall consider what an odd and unworthy piece of folly he hath committed.

Sir Thomas Browne

———

Christianity places the sexual instinct under a spiritual law, and permits its gratification only for the definite purpose of creating a Christian home.

Father Cuthbert

———

(Sex is) a trick to perpetuate the species.

Jerry Dashkin

———

The preservation of the species was a point of such necessity that nature has secured it at all hazards by immensely over-loading the passion, at the risk of perpetual crime and disorder.

Ralph Waldo Emerson

———

Sex. . .can be summed up in three P's: procreation, pleasure, and pride. From the long-range point of view, which we must always consider, procreation is by far the most important, since without procreation there could be no continuation of the race.

Madeline Gray

Only when husband and wife unite naturally is the union of sperm and ovum possible. Therefore the primary purpose of the marital act is in the conception of human life.

George A. Kelley

Amoebas at the start
  Were not complex,
They tore themselves apart
  And started Sex.

Arthur Guiterman

The union of the two sexes is meant only for the purpose of procreation in a man's lifetime, and the carnal affections are rendered legitimate by the production of children.

Lactantius

(Sex is) the formula by which one and one makes three.

Leonard L. Levinson

To enter life by way of the vagina is as good a way as any.

Henry Miller

The whole world depends on the holiness of the union between man and woman, for the world was created for the sake of God's glory and the essential revelation of His glory comes through the increase of mankind.

Rabbi Nahman of Bratslav

To reduce cohabitation and the conjugal act to a simple organic function for the transmission of seed would be converting the home, the sanctuary of the family, into a mere biological laboratory.

Pope Pius XII

The best prescription for a discontented female is to have a child.

Pablo Picasso

We have been God-like in our planned breeding of our domesticated plants and animals, but we have been rabbit-like in our unplanned breeding of ourselves.

Arnold Toynbee

Familiarity breeds contempt—and children.

Mark Twain

If you don't need any more babies, what do you need a family for?

Gore Vidal

Promiscuity

Make love to every woman you meet. If you get five percent on your outlay, it's a good investment.

Arnold Bennett

As bees their sting, so the promiscuous leave behind them in each encounter something of themselves by which they are made to suffer.

Cyril Connolly

It is a favorite neurotic misconception that a true adaptation to the world can be found by giving full rein to sexuality.

C. G. Jung

I've taken my fun where I've found it;
  I've rogued an' I've ranged in my time;
I've 'ad my pickin' o' sweethearts,
  An' four o' the lot was prime.

Rudyard Kipling

Promiscuous. . . . That was a word I had never applied to myself. Possibly no one ever does, for it is a sordid word, reducing many valuable moments to nothing more than dog-like copulation.

Marya Mannes

Eighty percent of married men cheat in America, the rest cheat in Europe.

Jackie Mason

Prostitution

The degree to which a pimp, if he's clever, can confuse and delude a prostitute is very nearly unlimited.

Polly Adler

A harlot repents as often as water turns to sour milk.

Arab proverb

The proliferation of massage establishments in London in the last few years appears to indicate a dramatic increase in muscular disorders amongst the male population.

Anonymous

The prostitute is the only honest woman left in America.

Ti-Grace Atkinson

Preferably I would not want my daughters in there, but not because I think it's wrong.

Joe Conforte (brothel owner)

No one was ever made wretched in a brothel.

Cyril Connolly

Sex is the great amateur art. The professional, male or female, is frowned on; he or she misses the whole point and spoils the show.

David Cort

A whore is like a crocodile that fastens upon her prey with her tail.

Samuel Butler

The commercial prostitution of love is the last outcome of our whole social system, and its most clear condemnation.

Edward Carpenter

Men will pay large sums to whores
For telling them they are not bores.

W.H. Auden

What men desire is a virgin who is a whore.

Edward Dahlberg

Prostitutes are the inevitable product of a society that places ultimate importance on money, possessions and competition.

Jane Fonda

A "prostitute" is a girl who knows how to give as well as take.

Xaviera Hollander

My method is basically the same as Masters and Johnson, only they charge thousands of dollars and it's called therapy. I charge fifty dollars and it's called prostitution.

Xaviera Hollander

———

There is only one other profession that outranks bankers as dedicated clients, and that is the stockbroker. . . . When the stocks go up, the cocks go up!

Xaviera Hollander

———

You can call me mercenary, or call me madam, but, as I always tell my customers—just call me anytime!

Xaviera Hollander

———

If my business was legitimate, I would deduct a substantial percentage for depreciation of my body.

Xaviera Hollander

———

. . .if my business could be made legal. . .I and women like me could make a big contribution to what Mayor Lindsay calls "Fun City," and the city and state could derive the money in taxes and licensing fees that I pay off to crooked cops and political figures.

Xaviera Hollander

———

Shy men of extreme sensibility are the born victims of the prostitute.

Christopher Isherwood

Since time immemorial, prostitutes have been the reward of men of action—soldiers, sailors, cowboys, gangsters—because whores are, above all else, women of action. Talk is not their stock in trade.

Brendan Francis

The work of the prostitute can be as routine and as boring as that in any other occupation.

Charles Winick and Paul M. Kinsie

No, no one sets out to be a madam; but madams answer the call of a well-recognized and very basic human need. Their responsibilities are thrust upon them by the fundamental nitwittedness and economic shortsightedness of most hustling broads. And they become tempered and sharpened and polished to the highest degree of professional awareness by constant intercourse with men devoutly dedicated to the policy of getting something for nothing.

Sally Stanford

The difference between the call girl and the courtesan. . . comes down to one word. Discipline.

Gail Sheehy

For me the madam life has become a big ego trip. I enjoy the independence and what's more, for me prostitution is not just a way to make a living, but a real calling, which I enjoy.

Xaviera Hollander

I've made so many movies playing a hooker that they don't pay me in the regular way any more. They leave it on the dresser.

Shirley MacLaine

=====

Prostitution is. . .the very core of the female's social condition. . . It is not sex the prostitute is really made to see: it is degradation.

Kate Millett

=====

Any good whore knows more about sex than Betty Friedan.

Sam Peckinpah

=====

I am not a slut, though I thank the gods I am foul.

Shakespeare

=====

It is a silly question to ask a prostitute why she does it. . . These are the highest-paid "professional" women in America.

Gail Sheehy

=====

There are a few good women who are not weary of their trade.

La Rochefoucauld

=====

If a woman hasn't got a tiny streak of a harlot in her, she's a dry stick as a rule.

D. H. Lawrence

Into this anonymous pit they climb—a fumbling, frightened, pathetic man and a cold, contemptuous, violated woman—prepared to exchange for twenty dollars no more than ten minutes of animal sex, untouched by a stroke of their common humanity.

Gail Sheehy

I've always had great respect for whores. The many I've known were kind and generous. . . . I never knew a prostitute who did harm to anyone but herself. I except, of course, the whores who are real criminals and use knockout drops and bring men to their rooms to be robbed, beaten, and blackmailed.

Ethel Waters

I've only hated men at those moments when I realized that I was doing all the giving and they the taking. At least when I was a prostitute, it was all honest and up front. No illusions and no lies about the relationships, which made it easier for both parties and made it possible for both parties to have a lot of fun—when they both liked what they were doing.

Xaviera Hollander

Prudery

Prudery is a form of avarice.

Stendhal

Aren't women prudes if they don't and prostitutes if they do?

Kate Millett

A good girl, whose grandmother would have refused to kiss her fiance until the engagement was sealed, now has to decide "how far to go" on each date to keep her reputation poised between prudish and loose.

Connie Brown

What is prudery?. . .
'Tis a virgin hard of feature,
Old and void of all good nature;
Lean and fretful; would seem wise,
Yet play the fool before she dies.

Alexander Pope

Puritanism

(Sex is) something that is often regulated by historical puritanism through law.

Rollo May

Our highly vaunted sexual freedom has turned out to be a new form of puritanism. I define puritanism as a state of alienation from the body, separation of emotion from reason, and use of the body as a machine.

Rollo May

For our highly repressive and Puritan tradition has almost hopelessly confused sexuality with sadism, cruelty, and that which is in general inhumane and antisocial. This is a deplorable state of affairs.

Kate Millett

For all of my patients sensuality is a giving in to "the low side of their nature." Puritanism is powerful and distorts their life with a total anesthesia of the senses. If you atrophy one sense you also atrophy all the others, a sensuous and physical connection with nature, with art, with food, with other human beings.

Anais Nin

The whole Puritan atmosphere has one advantage. . . It makes everything seem more exciting when you break away from it.

Viva

Purity

Purity of soul cannot be lost without consent.

Saint Augustine

I'm as pure as the driven slush.

Tallulah Bankhead

The body is the soul's image; therefore keep it pure.

Pope Xystus I

Women are constantly being given double messages: society preaches purity and the media portrays women as nothing but sex objects.

Ellen Frankfort

———

There's a woman like a dew-drop,
She's so purer than the purest.

Robert Browning

———

How like a lovely flower,
    So fair, so pure thou art;
I watch thee and a prayer
    Comes stealing through my heart. . .

Heinrich Heine

———

Oh! she was good as she was fair.
    None—none on earth above her!
As pure in thought as angels are;
    To know her was to love her.

Samuel Rogers

———

My good blade carves the casques of men,
    My tough lance thrusteth sure,
My strength is as the strength of ten,
    Because my heart is pure.

Alfred Lord Tennyson

———

I used to be snow white. . .but I drifted.

Mae West

253

R

Rape
Religion
Reputation
Resistance
Respect
Responsibility
Revenge
Romance

Rape

All men are rapists and that's all they are. They rape us with their eyes, their laws and their codes.

Marylin French

I find it absurd to assume that all coitus is rape. By saying that, one agrees to the masculine myth that a man's sex is a sword, a weapon.

Simone de Beauvoir

Among the porcupines, rape is unknown.

Gregory Clark

The master subjected her to the most elemental form of terrorism distinctly suited to the female: rape.

Angela Davis

Rape is not practiced among lower animals, but only among industrialized primates.

Ruth Herschberger

Rape has become a kind of favor done to the female—a fairly commonplace male fantasy.

Eleanor Perry

I found nothing grand in the history of the Jews nor in the morals inculcated in the Pentateuch. I know of no other books that so fully teach the subjection and degradation of women.
Elizabeth Cady Stanton

Religion

There is a tendency to think of sex as something degrading; it is not, it is magnificent, an enormous privilege, but, because of that, the rules are tremendously strict and severe. . . . It is easy to serve God in most other ways, but it is not so easy here.
Francis Devas

Religion has done love a great service by making it a sin.
Anatole France

Protestantism has contributed an obstacle to the fulfillment of legitimate sexual satisfaction whenever it has implied if not that sex is inherently evil, that it is at least repugnant and earthy.
Carl F. H. Henry

Judaism does not regard sexual union as a concession to the flesh but as a proper and sacred act.
Arthur Hertzberg

The union between the partners is transcendental. God has bound them together. Each party should love the Christ in the other. Every time intercourse occurs they do something holy.

Allen Keenan

Christian teaching about sex is by no means clear in detail, but what shines with pellucid clarity throughout the Christian tradition is that sex is a very holy subject.

Geddes MacGregor

As the French say, there are three sexes,—men, women, and clergymen.

Sidney Smith

If anything is sacred the human body is sacred.

Walt Whitman

Reputation

She was poor but she was honest
  And her parent was the same
Till she met a city feller
  And she lost her honest name.

Anonymous

Nothing is so delicate as the reputation of a woman; it is at once the most beautiful and most brittle of all human things.

Fanny Burney

The two things that a healthy person hates most between heaven and hell are a woman who is not dignified and a man who is.

G. K. Chesterton

Virtue in women is often merely love of their reputation and of their repose.

La Rochefoucauld

And one false step entirely damns her fame.
In vain with tears the loss she may deplore,
In vain look back on what she was before;
She sets like stars that fall, to rise no more.

Nicholas Rowe

No man can understand why a woman should prefer a good reputation to a good time.

Helen Rowland

Your women of honor, as you call'em, are only chary of their reputations, not their persons; and 'tis scandal that they would avoid, not men.

William Wycherley

Young ladies: You shouldn't go strolling about
When your anxious mamas don't know you are out;
And remember that accidents often befall
From kissing young fellows through holes in the wall.

J. G. Saxe

Resistance

Between a woman's Yes and No
There is not room for a pin to go.

Cervantes

A woman's resistance is no proof of her virtue; it is much more likely to be a proof of her experience. If we spoke sincerely, we should have to confess that our first impulse is to yield; we only resist on reflection.

Ninon D'Enclos

A pessimist is a man who thinks all women are bad. An optimist is one who hopes they are.

Chauncey Depew

Whether they give or refuse, it delights women to have been asked.

Ovid

Compose yourself Antonia. Resistance is unavailing, and I need to disavow my passion for you no longer. I possess you here alone; you are absolutely in my power, and I burn with desires which I must either gratify or die. My lovely girl! My adorable Antonia! Let me instruct you in joys to which you are still a stranger, and teach you to feel those pleasures in my arms, which I must soon enjoy in yours.

M. G. (Monk) Lewis

Respect

The woman who is resolved to be respected can make herself so even amidst an army of soldiers.

Cervantes

Men who cherish for women the highest respect are seldom popular with them.

Joseph Addison

There is no man who in his heart would not reverence a woman that chose to die rather than to be dishonored.

Thomas de Quincey

When a man gets up to speak, people listen, then look. When a woman gets up, people look; then, if they like what they see, they listen.

Pauline Frederick

The question is not if we *use* one another; the real question is do we *abuse* one another?

Arline M. Ruben

———

Honor women! they entwine and weave heavenly roses in our earthly life.

Johann von Schiller

———

I lose my respect for the man who can make the mystery of sex the subject of a coarse jest, yet, when you speak earnestly and seriously on the subject, is silent.

Henry David Thoreau

Responsibility

The marriage act ought not to be something roughly demanded or taken but something tenderly sought and mutually given, with each party realizing his or her obligation in justice to cooperate.

Charles Hugo Doyle

———

It is wrong to suggest that we favor depersonalized sex—unless, by depersonalized sex we are referring to any and all sexual activity that does not include extensive involvement, commitment and obligations. . .

Hugh Hefner

263

An attractive woman is one who is able to be committed, whether it's to career, art, or family.

Steve Bond

───

We were born in an era in which it was a disgrace for women to be sexually responsible. We matured in an era in which it was an obligation.

Janet Harris

───

Outside marriage, sexual intercourse is a self-giving without self-commitment, and hence is meaningless.

Richard A. McCormick

───

No man can be held throughout the day by what happens throughout the night.

Sally Stanford

───

The modern rule is that every woman must be her own chaperone.

Amy Vanderbilt

Revenge

If a man has sworn to injure you, you may sleep at night; if a woman, keep awake.

Arab proverb

After a quarrel between a man and a woman the man suffers chiefly from the thought that he has wounded the woman; the woman suffers from the thought that she has not wounded the man enough.

Friedrich Nietzsche

In revenge as in love woman is always more barbarous than man.

Friedrich Nietzsche

Romance

All a writer has to do to get a woman is to say he's a writer. It's an aphrodisiac.

Saul Bellow

Come, let us take our fill of love until the morning; let us solace ourselves with love. For the good of man is not at home, he is gone a long journey.

The Bible

Romantics, imagining how others feel after intercourse, report more euphoria and well-being than friendship-seekers do.

Keith E. Davis

Zephyr with Aurora playing,
As he met her once a-Maying,
There on beds of violets blue,
And fresh-blown roses wash'd in dew,
Fill'd her with thee, a daughter fair,
So buxom, blithe, and debonair.

John Milton

In the theatre, a hero is one who believes that all women are ladies, a villain one who believes that all ladies are women.

George Jean Nathan

S

Satisfaction

Seduction

Selfishness

Sex Education

Sexiness

Sexual Revolution

Sexuality

Shame

Sin

Singleness

Sleeping

Spontaneity

Sports

Submission

Substitution

Success, Sexual

Suffering

Superiority, Female

Superiority, Male

Satisfaction

Changing partners is such a thoroughly unspontaneous activity, so divorced from the vagaries of genuine sexual desire—no more than a variant on the square dance. In such a transaction sex is the sufferer: passion becomes lechery.

Germaine Greer

Sensuality is feared and oftentimes these people (surrogate program clients) go into situations very hurriedly and there's a lot of anxiety and the experience is bound to be doomed.

J. Smith
Professional sex surrogate

Men are so made that they can resist sound argument, and yet yield to a glance.

Honoré de Balzac

There are after all only two "rules" in good sex, apart from the obvious one of not doing things which are silly, antisocial or dangerous. One is "Don't do anything you don't really enjoy," and the other is "Find your partner's needs and don't balk them if you can help it."

Alex Comfort

(Sex is) finding the cool satisfaction of heaven in the heated embers of the pit.

Warren Goldberg

―――

The act (of sex is) gross and brief, and brings loathing after it.

Petronius

Seduction

Julia's voice was lost, except in sighs,
  Until too late for useful conversation;
The tears were gushing from her gentle eyes,
  I wish, indeed, they had not had occasion,
But who, alas! can love, and then be wise?
  Not that remorse did not oppose temptation;
A little still she strove, and much repented,
And whispering "I will ne'er consent"―consented.

George Gordon Byron

―――

Listen Bond, it'd take more than Crabmeat Ravigote to get me into bed.

Tiffany Case

―――

The harlot knows not how to love but only to ensnare; her kiss hath poison, and her mouth a pernicious drug.

John Chrysostom

There is nothing more shameful than to seduce an honest girl.
Wolfgang A. Mozart

Samson with his strong body had a weak head, or he would not have laid it in a harlot's lap.
Benjamin Franklin

The light that lies
In women's eyes,
Has been my heart's undoing.

Thomas Moore

Tonight, after the children are in bed, place a lighted candle on the floor and seduce him under the dining-room table.
Marabel Morgan

Women often wish to give unwillingly what they really like to give.

Ovid

I gutted your belly as I would a doll's
Examining its artifice of cogs
And buried deep within its golden pulleys
I found a trap bearing this label: sex.
Alfonsina Storni

A fox is a wolf who sends flowers.

Ruth Weston

Selfishness

The act of sex. . . is ruined today by. . .selfish pleasure seeking.

E. J. Gold

A man comes into the world with a loaf of bread in his hand; a woman comes into the world with both hands empty.

Hebrew proverb

The quintessence of every passion is selfishness.

Moritz Saphir

The best cure for hypochondria is to forget about your body and get interested in somebody else's.

Goodman Ace

Sex Education

Wherever social life has become more urban mobile and complex, the school has had to bridge this gap in learning that once was absorbed at the hearth.

Aron Krich

Experience must have taught educators that the task of moulding the sexual will of the next generation can only be carried out by beginning to impose their influence very early, and intervening in the sexual life of children before puberty, instead of waiting till the storm bursts.

Sigmund Freud

Like most women, most of what I knew about sex came from men.

Shere Hite

If sex and creativity are often seen by dictators as subversive activities, it's because they lead to the knowledge that you own your own body (and with it your own voice), and that's the most revolutionary insight of all.

Erica Jong

Sexual information without relation to values is intellectually irresponsible.

Peter A. Bertocci

We pray that the young men and women of today and tomorrow will grow up with the realization that sex is a beautiful flame they carry in the lantern of their bodies.

Demetrius Manousos

273

Everyone should study at least enough philosophy and belles lettres to make his sexual experience more delectable.

G. C. Lichtenberg

———

Far too common is the error of those who with dangerous assurance. . .propagate a so-called sex-education, falsely imagining they can forearm youth against the dangers of sensuality by means purely natural.

Pope Pius XI

———

Answering questions is a major part of sex education. Two rules cover the ground. First, always give a truthful answer to a question; second, regard sex knowledge as exactly like any other knowledge.

Bertrand Russell

———

From best-sellers to comic books, any child who hasn't acquired an extensive sex education by the age of 12 belongs in remedial reading.

Will Stanton

———

It is a privilege to help children and youth effect the transition from sexual ignorance, superstition, and immaturity to an enlightened, wholesome maturity and adulthood.

Alexander A. Schneiders

Once let the public become sufficiently clean-minded to allow every adult access to all that is known about the psychology, hygiene and ethics of sex, and in two generations we will have a new humanity, with more health and joy, fewer wrecked nerves, and almost no divorces.

Theodore Schroeder

Sexiness

Sexiness in a woman is certainly a redeeming social value.

Peter Bogdanovich

How to Be Sexy: Clean hair is sexy. . . Being able to sit very still is sexy. Smiles are sexy. It is unsexy to talk about members of your family and how cute or awful they are. Or about your boss a lot—he's another man. . .a rival. Talking all the time about anything is unsexy. Sphinxes and Mona Lisas knew what they were doing! Gossip—suprise, surprise—is not unsexy! . . . The little black dress is sexy. . . Perfume is sexy. Good health is sexy. Liking men is sexy. It is by and large just about the sexiest thing you can do. But I mean really liking, not just pretending. . . You must spend time plotting how to make him happier. Not just him. . .them!

Helen Gurley Brown

The woman who goes to bed with a man should put off her modesty with her skirt and put it on again with her petticoat.

Michel de Montaigne

———

When everything is linked to sex, it becomes difficult to determine and appreciate what is truly sexual. For sexiness is remote from sexuality. Sexiness remains very much on the surface in its distorted emphasis on the external aspects of human beings. To look sexy is not necessarily to be sexual. True sexuality is a function of the total personality, and is experienced and expressed only in the lives of truly mature people.

Eugene C. Kennedy

———

The reason people sweat is so they won't catch fire when making love.

Don Rose

———

Ma'am, ah'm not tryin' to be sexy. Ah didn't have any idear of trying to sell sex. It's just my way of expressin' how I feel when I move around. It's all leg movement. Ah don't do nothin' with my body.

Elvis Presley

———

She is sexy, witty, and dry-cleaned.

Mary Quant

Girls like me, and if that's sex appeal, I got it. But I don't know how to turn it on and turn it off. I don't walk around saying "hey, I got sex appeal."

Eddie Murphy

Sexual Revolution

Sexual liberation, as a slogan, turns out to be another kind of bondage. For a woman it offers orgasm as her ultimate and major fulfillment; it's better than motherhood.

Victoria Billings

One of the things still missing from the "new sexual freedom" is the unashamed ability to use sex as play—in this, psycho-analytic ideas of maturity are nearly as much to blame as old-style moralisms about what is normal or perverse. . . Play is one function of sexual elaboration—playfulness is a part of love which could well be the major contribution of the Aquarian revolution to human happiness.

Alex Comfort

Sexual freedom has become more important than identity. Indeed, it has superseded it. The modern philosophy states 'I ejaculate, therefore I am'.

Quentin Crisp

Women's Liberation calls it enslavement but the real truth about the sexual revolution is that it has made of sex an almost chaotically limitless and therefore unmanageable realm in the life of women.

Midge Decter

To some extent, sexual freedom has become confused with high levels of sexual performance. Both men and women have come to feel new pressure to meet these standards—and the pressures have proved destructive to the fundamental relationships.

Helen Singer Kaplan

Allowing for its crudities, the sexual revolution has been one of the few blessings in the life of this century.

V.S. Pritchett

The Sexual Revolution: Conquest of the last frontier, involving the efficient management and manipulation of reproductive organs for the purpose of establishing the New Puritanism.

Bernard Rosenberg

The back seat produced the sexual revolution.

Jerry Rubin

I worry about kids today. Because of the sexual revolution they're going to grow up and never know what dirty means.

Lily Tomlin

The so-called new morality is too often the old immorality condoned.

Lord Shawcross

Sexuality

Human sexuality is too noble and beautiful a thing, too profound a form of experience, to turn into a mere technique of physical relief, or a foolish and irrelevant pastime.

J.V.L. Casserley

What has been encouraged as healthy sexuality is but an expression of the brutal, fiendish rationalism (not reason) that harries love, and the relationship between man and woman has become one of the saddest commentaries of our time.

Ruth N. Anshen

Sexuality is the lyricism of the masses.

Charles Baudelaire

Man's brain has transformed the earth and the sea, but sensuality remains where it was before the flood. Women; wine, noise.

William Bolitho

In fact, eroticism often arrives as a late guest at its own banquet. A high degree of affection or rapport between two people, especially if they see each other across an otherwise unbridgeable barrier of age or status, can easily generate sexual feelings.

C.A. Tripp

If it is not erotic, it is not interesting.

Fernando Arrabal

At least some of the men who write sex books admit that they really don't understand female sexuality. Freud was one. Masters is another—that was why he got Johnson.

Arlene Croce

My own view, for what it's worth, is that sexuality is lovely, there cannot be too much of it, it is self-limiting if it is satisfactory, and satisfaction diminishes tension and clears the mind for attention and learning.

Paul Goodman

Contempt of sexuality is a crime against life.

Friedrich Nietzsche

The most powerful stimulant of sex is the effort to suppress it. There is only one cure—to take it up simply, frankly and naturally into the circle of our activities.

John MacMurray

Sex is a natural function like breathing or eating.

William Masters

Sex and sexuality never made anyone ill and never made anyone feel guilty. It is the hate and destructiveness concealed in them which produce strange aberrations and bitter regret.

Karl Menninger

There is no such thing as homosexual or heterosexual. . . We're so uptight about sensuality that the only people we can stroke as expressions of affection are children and dogs.

Kate Millett

Where my head is at now, expanding sexuality is not most satisfied through promiscuity but through continuously communicating with someone specifically.

Jack Nicholson

The degree and kind of a person's sexuality reach up into the ultimate pinnacle of his spirit.

Friedrich Nietzsche

Sexuality throws no light upon love, but only through love can we learn to understand sexuality.

Rosenstock-Huessy

———

For every woman who feels more aware of her body and aware of her role as a receiver of pleasure, there is also one man who feels inadequate because he cannot give the pleasure to the woman who demands it of him.

Jerry Schneiderman

Shame

Such is the way of an adulterous woman; she eateth and wipeth her mouth, and saith, I have done no wickedness.

The Bible

———

She is proud of catching male interest, of arousing admiration, but what revolts her is to be caught in return. With the coming of puberty she has become acquainted with shame; and the shame lingers on, mingled with her coquetry and her vanity.

Simone de Beauvoir

———

Nature is to be reverenced, not blushed at. It is lust, not the act itself, that makes sexual union shameful; it is excess, not the marital state as such, that is unchaste.

Tertullian

There are still in this country a tremendous number of people, even young people, who, the minute they get a sexual feeling with somebody, reach for the light switch, as if they are so ashamed of their own bodies. They don't want to see what's happening and they don't want to see their partner's body.

Don Fass

He who can await, the morning after, without dying of shame, the disdain of those fair eyes that have witnessed his limpness and impertinence. . .has never felt the satisfaction and pride of having conquered them and put circles around them by the vigorous exercise of a busy and active night.

Michel de Montaigne

Malice, like lust, when it is at its height, doth not know shame.

George Savile

All the Freudian system is impregnated with the prejudice which it makes it its mission to fight—the prejudice that everything sexual is vile.

Simone Weil

When you have found the place where a woman loves to be fondled, don't you be ashamed to touch it any more than she is.

Ovid

Sin

A woman will sometimes confess her sins, but I never knew one to confess her faults.

Josh Billings

Here's a rule I recommend: Never practice two vices at once.

Tallulah Bankhead

I have found that one big vice in a man is apt to keep out great many smaller ones.

Francis Bret Harte

'Tis the Devil inspires this evanescent ardor, in order to divert the parties from prayer.

Martin Luther

No passion or affection, with which we are born, can be in itself sinful: it becomes so, only by wilful or careless indulgence.

Jonathan Mayhew

Question: What kind of sins are the greatest? Answer: Adultery, fornication, murder, theft, swearing, witchcraft, sedition, heresies, or any the like.

John Bunyan

———

Sex without sin is like an egg without salt.

Luis Bunuel

———

Every sin is the result of a collaboration.

Stephen Crane

———

In man mortal sins are venial; in woman venial sins are mortal.

Italian proverb

———

The sin they do by two and two they must pay for one by one.

Rudyard Kipling

———

Draw not near to fornication; verily, it is ever an abomination, and evil is the way thereof.

The Koran

It is simpler to treat sex morally than reasonably. Moreover, believing in sin is a kind of tactful armor. A girl might find, in a given situation, that it is better to tell a young man that he was doing wrong than that he was being a social dunce. His self-esteem would suffer less.

Phyllis McGinley

Remorse is impotence, it will sin again. Only repentance is strong; it can end everything.

Henry Miller

We had taken the first step along the tortuous road that led to the sex war, sado-masochism, and ultimately to the whole contemporary snarl-up, to prostitution, prudery, Casanova, John Knox, Marie Stopes, white slavery, women's liberation, Playboy magazine, crimes passionels, censorship, strip clubs, alimony, pornography, and a dozen different brands of mania. This was the Fall. It had nothing to do with apples.

Elaine Morgan

It was not the apple on the tree, but the pair on the ground, I believe, that caused the trouble in the garden.

M.D. O'Connor

How many are there who do not sin from lack of desire or lack of occasion?

Joseph Roux

Well, there's a Book that says we're all sinners and I at least chose a sin that's made quite a few people happier than they were before they met me, a sin that's left me with very little time to consider other extremely popular moral misdemeanors, like usury, intolerance, bearing false tales, extortion, racial bigotry, and the casting of that first stone. And, I might add, a hell of a lot worse.

Sally Stanford

The husband's sin remains on the threshold, the wife's enters the house.

Russian proverb

Either the mysterious union of two human beings takes place in the sight of God or man flings himself away, surrenders his secret, delivers himself over to the flesh, desecrates and violates the secret of another, severs himself in a mysterious fashion from God.

Dietrich Von Hildebrand

The basic formula of all sin is: frustrated or neglected love.

Franz Werfel

To err is human, but it feels divine.

Mae West

Rabbi Joshua ben Levi said: "A man who knows that his wife fears heaven and does not fulfill his marital duty of cohabitation is to be called a sinner."

Yebamot

Singleness

A single woman's life is not particularly orderly. You have to take when the taking is good. . .the riotous living when it's offered, the quiet when there's nothing else. . . . You may marry or you may not. In today's world that is no longer the big question for women. . . . You, my friend, if you work at it, can be envied the rich, full life possible for the single woman today. It's a good show. . .enjoy it, from wherever you are, whether it's two in the balcony or one on the aisle— don't miss any of it.

Helen Gurley Brown

When we won the league championship, all the married guys on the club had to thank their wives for putting up with all the stress and strain all season. I had to thank all the single broads in New York.

Joe Namath

Girls who wear zippers shouldn't live alone.

John W. Van Druten

Sleeping

Explicitly sexual dreams, like wakeful sexual fantasies, are quite common. Seventy percent of females and nearly 100 percent of males have erotic dreams. (Kinsey et al., 1953).

Masters, Johnson, Kolodny

He sleeps fastest who sleeps alone.

Richard Avedon

No woman is worth the loss of a night's sleep.

Sir Thomas Beecham

Laugh and the world laughs with you, snore and you sleep alone.

Anthony Burgess

Spontaneity

When you start planning it and being deliberate about it, it goes wrong. It's usually just when you're both thinking about something else, or rather you're just preoccupied with other people, and boing! That's when it's all right. But you can't make that happen.

Nelson Algren

Male sexual response is far brisker and more automatic: it is triggered easily by things, like putting a quarter in a vending machine.

Alex Comfort

Gin a body meet a body
  Comin' thro' the rye,
Gin a body kiss a body,
  Need a body cry?

Robert Burns

For flavor, instant sex will never supersede the stuff you have to peel and cook.

Quentin Crisp

How to put the libido back, restore the lost spontaneity, drive, love of life, the individuality, that sex in America seems to lack?

Betty Friedan

Much of what makes people "click" sexually seems unexplainable except as chemistry. There's no way to force it to happen or to not deny it when it does.

Carol Lynn Mithers

A wise woman should never give herself for the first time by appointment—it should be an unforeseen delight.

Stendhal

Sports

The only reason I would take up jogging is so that I could hear heavy breathing again.

Erma Bombeck

He makes love like a footballer. He dribbles before he shoots.

John Cooper Clarke

I don't know why people like the home run so much. A home run is over as soon as it starts. . .wham, bam, thank you, ma'am. The triple is the most exciting play of the game. A triple is like meeting a woman who excites you, spending the evening talking and getting more excited, then taking her home. It drags on and on. You're never sure how it's going to turn out.

George Foster

Ever since the young men have owned motorcycles, incest has been dying out.

Max Frisch

I would still rather score a touchdown than make love to the prettiest girl in the United States.

Paul Hornung

Why don't you women stay home and be lovers and leave TV and football to the men?

> Head coach John Madden of the
> Oakland Raiders, denying CBS
> sportscaster Lee Arthur access
> to the practice field, 1972.

The only time sex has bothered me is when I do it during the competition.

> Bruce Jenner

Our society treats sex as a sport, with its record-breakers, its judges, its rules and its spectators.

> Susan Lydon

The human spirit sublimates
the impulses it thwarts;
a healthy sex life mitigates
the lust for other sports.

> Piet Hein

In any case, as long as more male passion, roughly calculated, goes into watching pro-football on television than into gently seducing the Mrs., and so long as the lady of the house secretly yearns for a tenderness she no longer seems to attract, the American ship of marriage sails near dangerous rocks.

> Michael Novak

I love football. I really love football. As far as I'm concerned, it's the second best thing in the world.

Joe Namath

Going to bed with a woman never hurt a ballplayer. It's staying up all night looking for them that does you in.

Casey Stengel

Submission

To see a patient and laborous female spending nearly her whole time in ministering to the mere physical wants of man, in the various shapes of his existence—infancy, childhood, youth, manhood and age—and doing all this with the utmost cheerfulness, and without appearing to realize that God has given her a higher and nobler office, is indeed most lamentable.

William A. Alcott (1852)

A man may brave opinion; a woman must submit to it.

Anna Louise de Staël

I am happy now that Charles calls on my bed chamber less frequently than of old. As it is I now endure but two calls a week and when I hear his steps outside my door I lie down on my bed, close my eyes, open my legs and think of England.

Lady Hillingdon

Vital ecstasy is self-surrender not to the other being as such but to the other being as far as it is the other side of the love-unity.

Paul Tillich

─────

It's really maddening to us as women to see young girls just lay themselves at the feet of any male who happens to be involved with rock'n'roll. It's a really sad sight, like sheep to the slaughter.

Ann Wilson

Substitution

Joy is not a substitute for sex, sex is very often a substitute for Joy. I sometimes wonder whether all pleasures are not substitutes for Joy.

C.S. Lewis

─────

The dream of college apparently serves as a substitute for more direct preoccupation with marriage: girls who do not plan to go to college are more explicit in their desire to marry, and have a more developed sense of their own sex role.

Elizabeth Douvan

─────

All dancing is a replacement for sex.

Mick Jagger

Success, Sexual

I know a lot of people didn't expect our relationship to last—but we've just celebrated our two months' anniversary.

Britt Ekland

===

If your life at night is good, you think you have everything; but, if in that quarter things go wrong you will consider your best and truest interests most hateful.

Euripides

===

Sexual congress in a Mailer novel is always a matter of strenuous endeavor, rather like mountain climbing—a matter of straining after achievement.

Kate Millett

===

Woman's vanity demands that a man be more than a happy husband.

Friedrich Nietzsche

Suffering

Men, the very best of men, can only suffer, while women can endure.

Dinah Mulock Craik

Women are infinitely fonder of clinging to and beating about, hanging upon and keeping up and reluctantly letting fall, any doleful or painful or unpleasant subject, than men of the same class and rank.

S.T. Coleridge

When rewards are distributed, the woman gets one half the pay that a man does, and if disgrace is given out she bears it all.

Elbert Hubbard

Mayhem, death and arson
Have followed many a thoughtless kiss
Not sanctioned by a parson.

Don Marquis

To those suffering from a broken relationship: Give yourself something you always wanted, not what you need. Indulge yourself in some way—it helps to restore your self esteem.

Lee Salk

A woman can be proud and stiff
When on love intent;
But Love has pitched his mansion in
The place of excrement;
For nothing can be sole or whole
That has not been rent.

William Butler Yeats

Superiority, Female

Girls have an unfair advantage over men: if they can't get what they want by being smart, they can get it by being dumb.

Yul Brynner

═══════

God made men stronger but not necessarily more intelligent. He gave women intuition and femininity. And, used properly, that combination easily jumbles the brain of any man I've ever met.

Farrah Fawcett-Majors

═══════

Let any woman, neither old nor ugly, and passing for modest, throw herself (as the phrase is) at any man's head she meets with, and she may set him down as her own from that time forward, unless he be either very wise or very stupid.

William Hazlitt

═══════

I don't mind the boys doing it, if they do it with their own class, but I won't have the girls doing it because they've got nothing to do it with.

Rosa Lewis

═══════

The females of all species are most dangerous when they appear to retreat.

Don Marquis

Love and respect woman. Look to her not only for comfort, but for strength and inspiration and the doubling of your intellectual and moral powers. Blot out from your mind any idea of superiority; you have none.

Joseph Mazzini

A caress is better than a career.

Elizabeth Marbury

Whether women are better than men I cannot say—but I can say they are certainly no worse.

Golda Meir

In the duel of sex, woman fights from the dreadnaught and man from an open raft.

H.L. Mencken

Women have served all these centuries as looking glasses possessing the. . .power of reflecting the figure of man at twice its natural size.

Virginia Woolf

Superliority, Male

All right, Edith, you go right ahead and do your thing. . .but just remember that your thing is eggs over-easy and crisp bacon.

Archie Bunker

We are still the property of men, the spoils today of warriors who pretend to be our comrades in the struggle, but who merely seek to mount us.

Maria Isabel Barreno

If a man has seduced a maiden on a promise of marriage, is he bound to keep his promise if he is much superior to the maiden in birth, and she was aware of that disparity? I think he is not the least bound.

Alphonsus Di Ligouri

The intelligence of woman is inferior to that of man, and every woman who tries to deny it proves it.

Diane de Poitiers

I may define man as a male human being and woman as a female human being. What the early Christians did was to strike the "male" out of the definition of man, and "human being" out of the definition of woman.

James Donaldson

Women have a less accurate measure of time than men. There is a clock in Adam: none in Eve.

Ralph Waldo Emerson

Women have a perpetual envy of our vices; they are less vicious than we, not from choice, but because we restrict them.

Samuel Johnson

The woman was not taken
  From Adams's head, we know,
To show she must not rule him—
  'Tis evidently so.
The woman she was taken
  From under Adam's arm,
So she must be protected
  From injuries and harm.

Abraham Lincoln

All the pursuits of men are the pursuits of women also, but in all of them a woman is inferior to a man.

Plato

Look you, I keep this house, and I wash, wring, brew, bake, scour, dress, eat and drink, make the beds, and do all myself. 'Tis a great charge to come under one body's hand.

Clarissa Packard

If the man is the head of the family, the woman is the heart, and as he occupies the chief place in ruling, so she may and ought to claim for herself the chief place in love.

Pope Pius XI

Men have more problems than women. In the first place, they have to put up with women.

Françoise Sagan

Man for the field and woman for the hearth;
Man for the sword, and for the needle she;
Man with the head, the woman with the heart;
Man to command, and woman to obey;
All else confusion.

Alfred Lord Tennyson

Man is the hunter; woman is his game:
The sleek and shining creatures of the chase,
We hunt them for the beauty of their skins;
They love us for it, and we ride them down.

Alfred Lord Tennyson

Male birds are almost always the wooers; and they alone are armed with special weapons for fighting with their rivals. They are generally stronger and larger than the females, and are endowed with the requisite qualities of courage and pugnacity.

Charles Darwin

Physically, a man is a man for a much longer time than a woman is a woman.

Honoré de Balzac

A male figure rises to the head, and is a symbol of the intelligence; a woman's figure sinks to the inferior parts of the body, and is expressive of generation.

George Moore

T

Talk, Sexy
Techniques
Temptation

Talk, Sexy

Women like silent men. They think they're listening.

Marcel Achard

Do not rush into your own bed after it. Talk a little bit, hang around.

Mel Brooks

Because of its secret nature, you should not talk or write about sex. You can have love talk with the person you're in love with—that's a different matter. But any talk of sex with others is anti-human.

Robert Graves

A woman never forgets her sex. She would rather talk with a man than an angel any day.

Oliver Wendell Holmes

When a woman is talking to you, listen to what she says with her eyes.

Victor Hugo

Ninety percent of a good sex life is being able to talk about sex. The other ten percent is actually doing it.

Marlene Janssen
Playboy Playmate

You must talk with each other, not just guess what your partner is thinking. What else are words for?

Hanna Kapit

Sex is a three-letter word which sometimes needs some old-fashioned four-letter words to convey its full meaning: words like help, give, care, love.

Sam Levenson

All really great lovers are articulate, and verbal seduction is the surest road to actual seduction.

Marya Mannes

We rarely talk of sex the way men do, in terms of I've had this one, I've had that one. There's a friend I've known for 19 years and all I've known of her private life is what I've heard from others. And yet our relation is very profound; if she dies, I die.

Jeanne Moreau

Like hatred, sex must be articulated or, like hatred, it will produce a disturbing internal malaise.

George Jean Nathan

You don't know a woman until you have had a letter from her.

Ada Leverson

His voice was as intimate as the rustle of sheets.

Dorothy Parker

Men are more eloquent than women made,
But women are more powerful to persuade.

Thomas Randolph

(Sex is) something that children never discuss in the presence of their elders.

Arthur S. Roche

It is better to be silent than to say things at the wrong time that are too tender; what was appropriate ten seconds ago is so no longer, and hurts one's cause, rather than helps it.

Stendhal

In Hollywood the favorite word is "sex"; in the Midwest it is "cheese"; in the South, "honey"; in Manhattan, "money."
Amy Vanderbilt

Techniques

If a woman doesn't chase a man a little, she doesn't love him.
E. W. Howe

Whoever named it necking was a poor judge of anatomy.
Groucho Marx

On a plane you can pick up more and better people than on any other public conveyance since the stagecoach.
Anita Loos

One of the hostess's duties is to act as a procuress.
Marcel Proust

I don't know what I am, dahling. I've tried several varieties of sex. The conventional position makes me claustrophobic. And the others give me either a stiff neck or lockjaw.
Tallulah Bankhead

Warren (Beatty) could handle women as smoothly as operating an elevator. He knew exactly where to locate the top button. One flick and we were on our way.

Britt Ekland

━━━━

Preoccupation with manipulative technique turns persons into objects, and touching is turned into the science of stimulation.

William H. Masters

━━━━

Any woman will love any man that bothers her enough.

Henry Wallace Phillips

━━━━

Last night I asked my husband, "what's your favorite sexual position" and he replied, "next door."

Joan Rivers

━━━━

Talk between lovers about techniques to improve sex is destructive in bed and constructive out of bed.

Theodore Isaac Rubin

━━━━

High in the art of living comes the wisdom of never letting anyone do anything for you until he is so anxious to do it that you know he is doing it with real joy.

David Seaburg

He that would win a maid must feign, lie, and
  flatter,
But he that woos a widow must down with his britches
  and at her.

Nathaniel Smith

I'm a fast-moving girl that likes them slow.

Mae West

When I'm good, I'm very good. But when I'm bad, I'm
better.

Mae West

It isn't what I do but how I do it. It isn't what I say but how I
say it. And how I look when I do it.

Mae West

Temptation

Woman is at once apple and serpent.

Heinrich Heine

I try never to be alone with a beautiful woman. Because,
when I'm alone, the devil in me becomes dangerous.

Tiny Tim

It is the people with secret attractions to various temptations who busy themselves with removing those temptations from other people; really they are defending themselves under the pretext of defending others because at heart they fear their own weaknesses.

Ernest Jones

Why resist temptation—there will always be more.

Don Herold

Don't worry about avoiding temptation—as you grow older, it starts avoiding you.

The Old Farmer's Almanac

Beauty and chastity are always quarreling.

Proverb

Virtue is insufficient temptation.

George Bernard Shaw

Union

Union

The creation of one flesh in the biblical sense involves the joining of two total existences, economically, spiritually, and psychologically, and not just the union of two bodies. To attempt the one without the other is dangerous to the entire relationship.

William G. Cole

The physical union of the sexes. . .only intensifies man's sense of solitude.

Nicolas Berdyaev

A bachelor gets tangled up with a lot of women in order to avoid getting tied up to one.

Helen Rowland

Sex cannot be contained within a definition of physical pleasure, it cannot be understood as merely itself for it has stood for too long as a symbol of profound connection between human beings.

Elizabeth Janeway

The Biblical revelation. . .does not limit the function of sexuality and the family to the reproductive purpose. Equally deeply rooted in Genesis is the reflection of a second factor—the need of man and woman for each other, to complement and fulfill each other and to establish a durable partnership against the loneliness and rigor of life.

Lambeth Conference

(Sex is) the sign that the lovers have nothing to refuse each other; that they belong wholly to each other.

Jacques Le Clercq

The monstrosity of sexual intercourse outside marriage is. . . trying to isolate one kind of union (the sexual) from all other kinds of union which were intended to go along with it and make up the total union.

C. S. Lewis

If the union of man and woman is the fruit of a love that is given in purity, generosity and fidelity, then the body itself is spiritualized in the service of a love that ennobles it, and, with God's blessing, sanctifies.

Jean Mouroux

In truth all experiences of the Divine Unity and Holiness depend on the union between man and woman, for the ultimate meaning of this act is very lofty.

Rabbi Nahman of Bratslav

Love grows, Lust wastes by Enjoyment, and the Reason is, that one springs from a Union of Souls, and the other from a Union of Senses.

William Penn

If sex does not mount to heaven it descends into hell. There is no such thing as giving the body without giving the soul. Those who think they can be faithful in soul to one another, but unfaithful in body, forget that the two are inseparable.

Fulton J. Sheen

A union of bodies is not the fullness of sexual union. It is valid only as an expression of the union of two personalities.

Fulton J. Sheen

A "perfect" partnership is one in which you and your partner not only respect each other's views, but you *understand* each other's views.

Adrian Warren

V

Vanity
Variety
Virginity
Virtue
Voyeurism
Vulnerability

Vanity

I shall never get used to not being the most beautiful woman in the room. It was an intoxication to sweep in and know every man had turned his head. It kept me in form.

Lady Randolph Churchill

A beautiful woman should break her mirror early.

Gracian

There are some girls who are turned on by my body and some others who are turned off. But for the majority I just use it as a conversation piece. Like someone walking a cheetah down Forty-Second Street would have a natural conversation piece.

Arnold Schwarzenegger

Woman's dearest delight is to wound man's self-conceit, though man's dearest delight is to gratify hers.

George Bernard Shaw

Variety

The human spirit wants to experience love in many ways, sex in many ways; adventure; probably destructiveness in many ways; jealousy too.

Shirley MacLaine

I believed that one woman was devoted to me, but she is now attracted by another man, and another man takes pleasure in her, while a second woman interests herself in me. Curses on them both, and on the god of love, and on the other woman, and on myself!

Bhartrihari

A woman talks to one man, looks at a second and thinks of a third.

Bhartrihari

Even a rat likes to go into a different hole once in a while.

Bohemian proverb

One man's mate is another man's passion.

Eugene Healy

Variety is the spice of sex.

Marabel Morgan

Variety is the soul of pleasure.

Aphra Behn

I keep saying I wish I had as much in bed as I get in the newspapers. I'd be real busy.

Linda Ronstadt

In the spring a young man's fancy lightly turns—and turns—and turns.

Helen Rowland

He who has one woman has all women; he who has all women has no woman.

Spanish proverb

Virginity

A virgin is like a rose growing in a garden, defended by its thorns, and safe from the shepard and his flock.

Ludovico Ariosto

A twenty-five-year-old virgin is like the man who was set upon by thieves—everyone passes by.

Charlotte Bingham

I believe absolutely in Christian sexual morality, which means that I believe in premarital virginity. Virgins don't get V.D., don't have abortions, don't have illegitimate babies, and aren't forced to get married. And no man, no matter how progressive, has ever objected to his bride being a virgin.

John Braine

The virgin. . .is not only an attribute of the body, it is a state of mind.

Barbara Cartland

Every man has been brought up with the idea that decent women don't pop in and out of bed; he has always been told by his mother that 'nice girls don't.' He finds, of course, when he gets older that this may be untrue; but only in a certain section of society. The great majority of people in England and America are modest, decent and pure-minded and the amount of virgins in the world today is stupendous.

Barbara Cartland

So a maiden, while she remains untouched, remains dear to her own; but when she has lost her chaste flower with sullied body, she remains neither lovely to boys nor dear to girls.

Catullus

You see me with child, and you want me a virgin.

Cervantes

Are there still virgins? One is tempted to answer no. There are only girls who have not yet crossed the line, because they want to preserve their market value. . . . Call them virgins if you wish, these travelers in transit.

Françoise Giroud

All females are born virgin and may die virgin. Virginity is eternal.

R. Buckminster Fuller

She who keeps chastely to her husband's side
Is not for one but every night his bride;
And stealing still with love and fear to bed,
Brings him not one, but many a maidenhead.

Robert Herrick

I will say it boldly, though God can do all things. He cannot raise a virgin up after she has fallen.

Saint Jerome

I knew her before she was a virgin.

Oscar Levant

Nature abhors a virgin—a frozen asset.

Clare Boothe Luce

Virginity is peevish, proud, idle, made of self-love, which is the most inhibited sin in the canon.

Shakespeare

By no art can chastity, once injured, be made whole.

Ovid

How rare a thing it is to match virginity with beauty.

John Lyly

Virtue

Most plain girls are virtuous because of the scarcity of opportunity to be otherwise.

Maya Angelou

Not that I mistrust her virtue, but—she is a woman. There lies the suspicion.

Rabelais

Nothing so splinters the self as a bed shared with an unknown body.

Jack Richardson

As long as the sexual act itself corresponds to the rational order, the abundance of pleasure does not conflict with the proper mean of virtue . . . And even the fact that reason is unable to make a free act of cognition of spiritual things simultaneously with that pleasure does not prove that the sexual act conflicts with virtue.

Saint Thomas Aquinas

Be good, even at the cost of your self-respect.

Don Herold

Who can find a virtuous woman? for her price is far above rubies.

The Bible

A virtuous woman is a crown to her husband.

The Bible

Blessed is the man that hath a virtuous wife, for the number of his days shall be double. A virtuous woman rejoiceth her husband, and he shall fulfil the years of his life in peace.

The Bible

If venereal delight and the power of propagating the species were permitted only to the virtuous, it would make the world very good.

James Boswell

There is no charm in the female sex that can supply the place of virtue. Without innocence, beauty is unlovely, and quality contemptible, good-breeding degenerates into wantonness, and wit into impudence.

Eustache Budgell

As to virtue. . .it is an act of the will, a habit which increases the quantity, intensity and quality of life. It builds up, strengthens and vivifies personality.

Alexis Carrel

Once a woman parts with her virtue, she loses the esteem even of the man whose vows and tears won her to abandon it.

Cervantes

Rare are those who prefer virtue to the pleasures of sex.

Confucius

The English laws punish vice; the Chinese laws do more. They reward virtue.

Oliver Goldsmith

Any of us can achieve virtue, if by virtue we merely mean the avoidance of the vices that do not attract us.

Robert S. Lynd

Virtue is an intellectual force of the soul which so rules over animal suggestions or bodily passions that it easily attains that which is absolutely and simply the best.

Henry Moore

And virtue flies when love once blows the sail.

Shackerbley Marmion

When we are planning for posterity, we ought to remember that virtue is not hereditary.

Thomas Paine

Most good women are hidden treasures who are only safe because nobody looks for them.

Dorothy Parker

When men grow virtuous in their old age, they only make a sacrifice to God of the devil's leavings.

Alexander Pope

For women are as roses, whose fair flower
Being once display'd, doth fall that very hour.

Shakespeare

Woman's virtue is man's greatest invention.

Cornelia Otis Skinner

Lord, what fine notions of virtue do we women take up upon the credit of old foolish philosophers! Virtue's its own reward, virtue's this, virtue's that—. Virtue's an ass, and a gallant's worth forty on't.

John Vanbrugh

Be virtuous and you will be eccentric.

Mark Twain

Voyeurism

Voyeurism is a healthy, non-participatory sexual activity—the world should look at the world.

Desmond Morris

A good stripper thinks of her audience as one man whose sexual appetite she's going to whet and whose fantasies she's going to satisfy.

Fanne Fox

Striptease has always been a display of the power of suggestion.

Fanne Fox

Vulnerability

Men who do not make advances to women are apt to become victims to women who make advances to them.

Walter Bagehot

Every man is to be had one way or another, and every woman almost any way.

Lord Chesterfield

A woman that loves to be at the window is a bunch of grapes on the highway.

English proverb

Give God thy broken heart, He whole will make it:
Give woman thy whole heart, and she will break it.

E. Prestwich

. . . in the position of a virgin washed ashore on a Devil's Island of convicted rapists.

Mario Puzo

Willingness

Wisdom

Woman

Women's Liberation

Willingness

The spirit indeed is willing, but the flesh is weak.

The Bible

Every maiden's weak and willin'
When she meets the proper villain.

Clarence Day

Theologians have always recognized that passions may overwhelm the person suddenly and completely to the point where freedom of choice does not exist and responsibility is not present.

J. Dominian

You know women as well as I do. They are only willing when you compel them, but after that they're as enthusiastic as you are.

Jean Giraudoux

Our world has changed. It's no longer a question of "Does she or doesn't she?" We all know she wants to, is about to, or does.

"J" (Joan Garrity)

To say why gals act so or so,
  Or don't, 'ould be presumin';
Mebby to mean yes an' say no
  Comes natural to women.

J. R. Lowell

No is no negative in a woman's mouth.

Philip Sidney

Adultery is an evil only inasmuch as it is a theft; but we do not steal that which is given to us.

Voltaire

Wisdom

Experience increases our wisdom but doesn't reduce our follies.

Josh Billings

Women are wiser than men because they know less and understand more.

James Stephens

Even the wisest men make fools of themselves about women, and even the most foolish women are wise about men.

Theodor Reik

Woman

There are lots of good women who, when they get to heaven, will watch to see if the Lord goes out nights.

Ed Howe

Variability is one of the virtues of a woman. It obviates the crude requirements of polygamy. If you have one good wife you are sure to have a spiritual harem.

G. K. Chesterton

To be a real woman is to bring out the best in a man.

Sandra Dee

When a woman behaves like a man, why doesn't she behave like a nice man?

Dame Edith Evans

The next woman that comes to you—look at her with new eyes. Treat her first as a person, not as a young woman. For that, I think, is essentially what the new image of woman is: a person first, a woman second. Think about it and then change your image of women.

Arvonne S. Fraser

Despite my thirty years of research into the feminine soul, I have not yet been able to answer. . .the great question that has never been answered: What does a woman want?

Sigmund Freud

We women were designed to delight, excite and satisfy the male of the species.

"J" (Joan Garrity)

She knifed me one night 'cause I wished she was white,
And I learned about women from 'er!

Rudyard Kipling

The Eternal Feminine draws us upward.

Johann W. von Goethe

Only the woman of the world is a woman; the rest are females.

Edmond and Jules de Goncourt

Women are not much, but they are the best other sex we have.

Don Herold

All that remains of her now is pure womanly.

Thomas Hood

A turtle is like a woman. You can't tell by its build how it's going to move.

Doug McNair

It is only a man here and there who has any tolerable knowledge of the character even of the women of his own family.

J. S. Mill

Woman learns how to hate in the degree that she forgets how to charm.

Friedrich Nietzsche

A real woman is a young, pretty, sexy, tender woman who is no taller than five feet six who adores you.

Françoise Parturier

Chaste to her husband, frank to all beside,
A teeming mistress, but a barren bride.

Alexander Pope

Every man wants a woman to appeal to his better side, his nobler instincts and his higher nature—and another woman to help him forget them.

Helen Rowland

A man's ideal woman is the one he passes with a worshipful bow—when he's on his way to call on the other woman.

Helen Rowland

Part of the role of being female in this Western society is the fact that a woman is allowed to feel more. . .she's the weaker sex, supposedly, because she feels. The big thing in our society is holding back and separating yourself from feeling.

Tina Russell

Frailty, thy name is woman.

Shakespeare

In the beginning, said a Persian poet,—Allah took a rose, a lily, a dove, a serpent, a little honey, a Dead Sea apple, and a handful of clay. When he looked at the amalgam—it was a woman.

William Sharp

I don't want to be kept as somebody's little pet. I'm smart.

Deborah Shelton

Woman is as false as a feather in the wind.

F. M. Piave

To be sure he's a "Man," the male must see to it that the female be clearly a "Woman," the opposite of a "Man,"that is, the female must act like a faggot.

Valerie Solanis

It would be difficult for me to say I'm against working women when I've had a Champagne Lady on my show for nineteen years. . .I like clean ladies and nice ladies.

Lawrence Welk

Women's Liberation

One of the trump cards that men who are threatened by women's liberation are always dredging up is the question of whether there is sex after liberation.

Nora Ephron

How can a man be sentimental, caring, and gentle when today's woman is so aggressive? Why, we men might end up in the kitchen.

Bob Fenton

Women get more unhappy the more they try to liberate themselves.

Brigitte Bardot

So cry not for the Ferraro candidacy. Nobody lost by it. The women were in the kitchen when the thing started, and they're in the kitchen where they belong here at the end of it.

Jimmy Breslin

Instead of fulfilling the promise of infinite orgastic bliss, sex in the America of the feminine mystique is becoming a strangely joyless national compulsion, if not contemptuous mockery.

Betty Friedan

Sex is the only frontier open to women who have always lived within the confines of the feminine mystique.

Betty Friedan

The only alliance I would make with the Women's Liberation Movement is in bed.

Abbie Hoffman

In many ways the failure of the E.R.A. has so pricked the conscious of the males who defeated it that they're learning more from having voted wrong.

Shirley MacLaine

Prehistoric man dealt with women's liberation quite well with his club.

Rodney Mansfield

===

To be successful, a woman has to be much better at her job than a man.

Golda Meir

===

No woman can call herself free who does not own and control her body. No woman can call herself free until she can choose consciously whether she will or will not be a mother.

Margaret Sanger

===

Can man be free if woman be a slave?

Percy Bysshe Shelley

===

The prejudice against color, of which we hear so much, is no stronger than that against sex. It is produced by the same cause and manifested very much in the same way. The Negro's skin and the woman's sex are both prima facie evidence that they were intended to be in subjection to the white Saxon man.

Elizabeth Cady Stanton

===

A liberated woman is one who has sex before marriage and a job after.

Gloria Steinem

Sexual freedom (for women) can be an excellent instrument for the expression of neurotic drives arising outside the strictly sexual sphere, especially drives expressive of hostility to men, or of the desire to be a man. Thus promiscuity may mean the collecting of scalps with the hope of hurting men, frustrating them, or taking away their importance, or in another case it may mean to the woman that she is he—a man.

Clara Thompson

Index

346